THIS BOOK IS DEDICATED TO MY DEAR LOVING PARENTS, **MARIE & ANGELO POLITO**: THE TRUE EDUCATORS! THANK YOU FOR THE GIFT OF LIFE, IT IS UP TO ME TO LIVE IT!

THIS BOOK IS FOR YOU IF:

- You're looking to improve your eating habits.

- You're a vegetarian or a gluten-free eater.

- You want to eat healthy, balanced meals.

- You want easy-to-prepare, timesaving meals with little clean up.

- You want to lose weight and learn how the body processes food.

- You're interested in delicious and artful dishes.

Hi Simon
Eat well!
Tony

To Contact **Tony Polito**
tony@cookingwithtony.com

THANK YOU FOR PURCHASING THIS COOKBOOK.

I HOPE TO ENHANCE THE LIVES OF OTHERS THROUGH COOKING WITH FRESH FOODS.

ESTABLISHING AND MAINTAINING A HEALTHY DIET STARTS IN THE KITCHEN. EACH RECIPE IN THIS BOOK SPOTLIGHTS HEALTH, NUTRITION AND IS CENTERED ON PROPER DIGESTION.

THIS BOOK WAS DESIGNED AS A TRANSITIONAL BOOK TO A HEALTHIER WAY OF EATING AND ISN'T MEANT TO BE A "DIET" BOOK.

WORD FROM TONY
EATING HEALTHY NEVER TASTED SO GOOD

Quick Tips

.................................7-21

Breakfast

Avocado Omelet with Pea Sprouts 23

Crunchy Almond Butter Snack 24

Ruby Red Grapefruit & Pear
with Ginger Sauce 27

Toasty, Sweet Onion Egg White Sandwich ..28

Shakes

Banana & Blueberry Shake 33

Banana & Strawberry Shake
with Cacao Nibs 34

Passionate Mango Smoothie 37

Strawberry Shake..38

Soups

Chunky Tomato Soup 43

Fresh & Simple Cannellini Bean Soup 44

Not-So-Classic Minestrone Soup 47

Strawberry Summer Soup 48

Salads

Baby Spinach with Avocado & Chickpeas ...53

Butternut Squash
with Baby Romaine Lettuce 54

Crispy Salad with Lemon Pepper Dressing .57

Field Greens
with Burdock Root & Goat Cheese 58

Minty Red Cabbage Salad 61

Miso Hungry Dressing 62

Nutty Spring Salad
with Lemon & Lime Dressing 65

Sweet Dandelion Salad with Sprouts 66

Tangy Dijon Mustard Salad 69

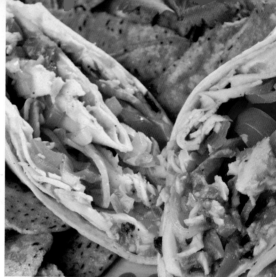

Sandwiches

Avocado & Goat Cheese on Ezekiel 73

Baby Spinach Smoked Turkey Wrap 74

Crispy Ciabatta
with Prosciutto & Mozzarella 77

Crunchy Pesto Veggie Panini 78

Green Leafy Wrap with Smoked Salmon ...81

Hummus Wrap with Sautéed Veggies 82

Not-Your-Average Ham and Cheese 85

Pa' volver a Comer 86

Portobello Shiitake Wrap
with Sweet Onions 89

Toasted Panini with Avocado & Cheese 90

Smoked Salmon with Cheese 93

Pasta

Butternut Ravioli with Parmigiano 97

Butternut Sage Sauce 98

Cheese Ravioli
with Creamy Delicata Shavings 101

Creste di Gallo with Pesto 102

Organic Ravioli with Broccoli Florets 105

Turkey Sausage with Ravioli 106

Wicked Fast Tomato Sauce 109

Fish

Citrus Salmon with Greens 113

Citrus Simmered Scallops
with Baby Greens 114

Savory Summer Sole
with a Ricotta Filling 117

Seared Tuna
with Cashew Crusted Topping 118

Seared Tuna with Walnut Puree 121

Meat

Boneless Pork Loin
with Pomegranate Sauce 125

Chicken with Garlic & Swiss Chard 126

Earthy Veal Cutlet 129

Feta Spinach Chicken Sausage
with Veggies 130

Sautéed Filet Mignon
with Peppery Parsnips 133

Turkey Sausage with Collard Greens 134

Side Dishes

Asparagus
with Creamy Strawberry Tomatoes 139

Cheesy Toasted Bread 140

Creamy Leeks with Baby Spinach 143

Crunchy Pistachio Beet Salad 144

Dynamite Edamame 147

Elegant Eggplant Appetizer 148

Fresh Sweet Basil with Ripe Tomatoes 151

Basic Homemade Hummus 152

Jazzed Up Potato Chips 155

Port Wine Drizzle 156

Sautéed Broccoli Rabe with Garlic 159

Shiitake Bruschetta with Vidalia Onions 160

Succulent Tomato Snack 163

Sweet Peppers with Swiss Chard 164

Crunchy Zucchini with Onions 167

Desserts

Apple Sauce 171

Banana Boat
with Spiced Blueberry Puree 172

Ice Cold Watermelon with Lemon Juice 175

Mango Tango Dessert 176

Pineapple Spilt with Meyer Lemons 179

Honey Figs
with Pineapple & Mango Purée 180

Smooth & Sweet Blueberry Pudding 183

Sour Apple Treat 184

Sweet Minty Trio...187

Very Berry Delight 188

Warm Apple Banana Dessert 191

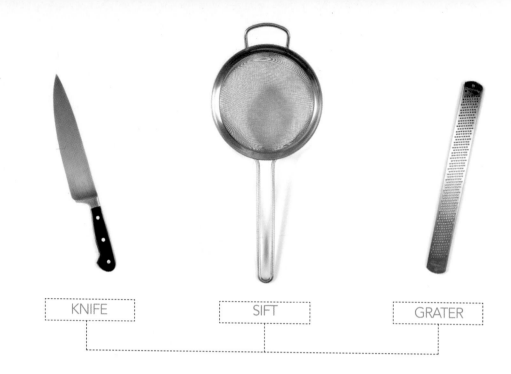

KNIFE

SIFT

GRATER

EVERYTHING YOU NEED TO START COOKING

10" PAN

CUISINART

MANDOLIN

QUICK
HEALTHY COOKING

Who has time to spend more than 10 minutes in the kitchen these days? Most people don't. As a result, they struggle with getting the right balance of healthy foods in their diets. If you're anything like me, sometimes it can be difficult to find time to make a quick, easy, healthy and inexpensive meal.

In this book you will find healthy and delicious dishes that you can prepare in under 10 minutes. Even better, each dish can be completed with, at most, six tools from your kitchen. And, you'll find that most of the recipes make use of a food processor for cutting, chopping, mincing, and dicing which saves a lot of time (and maybe your fingertips!)

There are even some quick tips on how to dress up your 10-minute dish so it looks as if you spent much longer on it! What's more, each dish tastes incredible and is designed so that your body gets the most out of it. If you learn to make every recipe in this book, I guarantee you'll become an extraordinary cook!

Nutrition

Price Tag on Your Health

Trip to store for one of Tony's recipes.......$10
Staying within your serving size $10
Eating healthier meals…….............Priceless

There's a cost to everything - we all know that. But there's a rule that I always keep in mind about food, "cheap can be double the price on the body". Consider the fast food burger - is it really that cheap? At $3.00, you might think so, but at 650 calories and approximately 50 grams of saturated fat, it is actually very expensive for your body in that it costs a lot of energy to digest. Fast food isn't fast when it comes to digestion! When your body finally manages to break that burger down, it finds that there is very little nutrition available for your body to use.

Along with each recipe, you'll find nutrition facts to enable you to keep tabs on the value of what you are consuming. In addition, you will also find tips on how to read labels to ensure that you are buying foods that help ease digestion and fuel your body, while avoiding those that are harmful.

You may think that reading labels and carefully selecting ingredients sounds like a lot of work, but it really doesn't have to be. It is important to know exactly what you are consuming. For example, if you look at the total fat on a nutrition label, you may think, "Oh that's nothing, I can eat that." However, not all fats are created equal! Take a closer look at the different types of fats that make up total fat content. The label often only tells part of the story. Knowing and identifying which ingredients make up the food is just as important. Refer to the chart at the back of the book for a better understanding of the nutrition labels.

Making the Right Choices

We all know what to eat when we are sick. I've asked some children, "What do you eat or drink when you're sick?" They replied, "I eat soup, drink tea, sleep, and stay home from school." I think that it's pretty ironic that we take special care to make the right choices when we don't feel well, but take far less care when we do feel well. When sick, we don't order pizza, eat hamburgers, chomp down candy bars or stay up until the wee hours. When we're sick, what do we do? We consume more greens, drink more herbal tea, and minimize soda, milk, coffee and alcohol. Suddenly, sleep becomes a priority. If we practice these healthy behaviors when we are well, our bodies will be on their way to becoming stronger and more enabled to fight disease. Your intelligence will supersede your taste buds and cravings, and you'll be on your way to making better choices!

Setting Up Your Kitchen

I recommend the following six tools to have in your kitchen's arsenal:

1) **Good quality knife**
   (cost varies, so get the best you can afford)

2) **Food processor** (around $40)

3) **Mandolin** (around $30)

4) **Stainless steel mesh strainer**
   (around $20 for an 8"strainer)

5) **Stainless steel zester or box cheese grater**
   (around $10)

6) **Skillet** (around $50 for an 8" or larger size)

In total, that's less than $200. Cooking will be much easier and more enjoyable from now on because you'll have fabulous and durable tools. The one item on the list that you might prefer to buy offline would be the knife. I'd suggest you aim to buy a knife that feels natural in your hand.

A food processor will save you a lot of cutting, but the downside is that it has a lot of parts, which means – you guessed it – a lot of washing. Typically when I'm preparing a meal, I use the food processor a number of times for different ingredients without worrying about cleaning out the bowl in between each use. This saves time and energy. When finished, I rinse the parts and stick them in the dishwasher and let the machine take care of it.

TONY TIPS
Modeling Dough vs. Bread

If you aren't feeling well, the first thing I'd recommend would be to stop eating bread. Most bread is just one ingredient away from being Modeling Dough. Therefore, it is difficult for the body to digest, especially when it is already congested with illness. Bread supplies few nutrients to your body and potentially be stored as fat if it is not burned after consumption.

When looking at mandolins, (a hand-held utensil with a blade for slicing and shredding), I would recommend the Benriner Japanese mandolin. Over the years, I've found that it's the best one to use. It's one of the most essential cutting tools in my kitchen, and can be used for a variety of chopping needs.

I could not live without a strainer. It's the most underrated utensil in the kitchen. I typically use it for removing water from my dishes as well as straining some of my favorite soups and desserts.

A stainless steel zester is a simple type of grater that is another essential tool in my kitchen. The brand I use is Microplane. Many folks don't have one of these, but they are as useful as a screw driver. Though extremely sharp, this utensil is much safer than regular graters because you're less likely to lose your grip or fingers. It can be used for grating various types of food, such as lemons, limes, nuts, hard cheeses and cookies.

When buying a skillet, you want to look for an 18/10 Stainless Steel skillet. "18/10" refers to the metals the skillet is made from: 18% chromium and 10% nickel. This is the perfect combination for efficient, even heating. All-Clad is my favorite brand, but Cuisinart or one of the other major store brands is also recommended.

To Heat or Not to Heat?

Be careful to preserve your food's natural flavors by not overcooking. I use a highly effective technique to prevent burning - taking food off the heat. Everyone's oven is different, whether it's electric or natural gas. So keep in mind that during the cooking process you might need more liquid, that is, more broth, water or whatever you choose. If one of my recipes says, "cook for six minutes," your stove might cook it in four minutes. Rather than adding more oil, try turning down the heat or removing the skillet from the stove completely. Over-cooking food is not cool! Remember, you want nutrients in your food to be broken down in your digestive tract, not in the pan!

Eating and Emotions

Eat when you're happy, not when you're angry or upset. Seriously! Avoid eating when you've just finished a yelling marathon with a loved one. It's an easy way to get started towards improving your health - and its free! If you feel upset, stressed, or outright mad, it doesn't matter if you're eating organic sprouts with wheatgrass juice or a Twinkie with popcorn and soda. Negative thoughts can have a dramatic and instantaneous effect on your body's digestion. Thoughts and energy absolutely affect your physiology and overall health.

If you're tight for time and can't wait until you feel better to eat, try to gather your thoughts and channel your stress and energy into a more positive disposition. So, before you think about changing your diet, first consider being more conscious of how you eat and how you feel when you're eating. Then you can move on to what you're eating.

Your body will fight for its own wellbeing and will use every fiber it has to stay healthy, so help it do its job! Give yourself enough time between meals to grow hungry, and then consider your thoughts and what enters your mind before considering what enters your mouth.

Digestion

Diet is about what you eat, how you eat, when you eat, and what you excrete. It's called a restroom for a reason, you simply rest, it's not Gold's Gym - no exercise should be required. When thinking of white flour and digestion, I picture the flour as being similar to the clothing lint that's collected in the filter of the dryer. Imagine the dryer filter as your stomach. It's filthy after just one use. If you don't clean the screen out, it just builds up and builds up and then one day, BAM! Your dryer overheats. If that was your body, you'd become sick. If you choose to frequently eat white breads and pastas, take this analogy into consideration. Also, be sure to only eat them in the recommended serving size. Give your body time to digest them and break them down before eating another serving.

Chewing

Chewing your food the right way is essential to good digestion, and therefore, good nutrition. Did you know it takes 15 to 20 minutes for our brain to realize our stomach is full? This is so important! Food needs to be fully chewed and eaten slowly. One way to get yourself to slow down is to focus on really enjoying the taste of your food while you're eating.

Don't just rip, tear and swallow your food. The key to proper eating is to make food absorbable. This means that one way you can improve your health without changing your diet is to dissolve your food properly. Think of your mouth as being a food processor, and puree your food while you eat.

Think of it this way, if you don't use your car, do you keep filling it up with fuel? Based on your physical activities during the day, your body might desire more or less water or food than on other days. Eat and drink accordingly. Try to listen to your body. First, wait until you're hungry. Second, think about what you've had to drink lately to determine if you might be dehydrated - feeling hungry doesn't necessarily mean you need food, it might mean you need water and are not actually hungry! Sometimes drinking a glass of water will allow hunger pains to subside. The old adage, "drink 8 glasses of water a day" can still hold water. Third, eat small amounts. Fourth, if you feel hungry, wait for 15 minutes, and then eat. Fifth, try not to skip meals. When people get wrapped up in their day-to-day activities and skip meals, they become fatigued more quickly, run out of fuel and often find that when they finally do eat, they overeat. The better option is to eat more often and in smaller quantities.

Eating smaller amounts of food, eating smaller portions and eating slowly are three habits that can dramatically help you attain your healthy eating goals. Our bellies are the size of our fists. Any portion that is bigger than one's hand is too much. It's that simple! You don't need any special measures, scales, units, or tools; just your hand is required.

Choosing Oils

Extra virgin olive oils sold in small bottles are best. It's not necessary to purchase gallons and gallons to store at home. Extra virgin olive oils that are sold in large quantities can sometimes have canola oil mixed in. The shelf life of an opened bottle of extra virgin olive oil is about two to three months, after which, it can become rancid. Unfortunately, you won't know that by the taste, because your taste buds won't pick it up… but it will smell like old French fries!

"Canola" is actually an abbreviation for Canadian Oil Low Acidity, and it is made from rapeseed. It's not bad for you, but it is oil your body can live without. Canola oil is tasteless, and has the crafty ability to mimic the flavor of any other oil with which it's blended. For example, canola oil is often blended in with the most expensive and most flavorful oil of all - truffle oil. If you purchase truffle oil, use the same approach as I discussed for extra virgin olive oils - buy as close to the real thing as possible. If you already have canola oil, keep it around the house - it's great for door jams and creaky window panes!

Cooking Oils

Whenever I think of quality extra virgin olive oil, I think of all the people who heat it.

In general, heating oils is not a good idea. Think of it this way: if you were going to rob a bank, you'd certainly rob a bank that had money. If you're going to cook with oil, use oil that can take the heat, baby! Since oils break down at different temperatures, certain oils are much better to heat than others. The oils I cook with regularly are sunflower oil, safflower oil, and occasionally peanut oil. These oils sometimes even say "high heat" on the bottle. You'll never see an extra virgin olive oil that reads "high heat." What it will say is, "cold pressed".

TONY TIPS
Canola Oil In Recipes

Anytime you see canola oil in a recipe, you can use safflower or sunflower oil as an alternative, even in baking. I've done it many times, and can testify that it works very well. Not to worry though, you will never see canola oil used in one of the recipes in this book.

TONY TIPS

Olive Oil Tasting!

If you want to have fun with a date, go olive oil tasting! It's one way to get a wealth of knowledge while not spending a lot of cash. After you've been to one, you could even host your own tasting session with a few friends.

Sunflower and safflower oils have higher heat tolerances than others and therefore, are better suited for heating and frying (though I would rather you not fry your foods. But if you are going to fry, use one of these oils instead).

Three major enemies of extra virgin olive oil are air, heat and light. These factors will cause it to become rancid over time. Olives are actually fruits, so their oils are part of their juices. When purchasing this beautiful fruit juice, it's best to buy it in dark green bottles that will protect the oil from UV light. If you love a particular oil that comes in a clear bottle, dig for the bottle that's nestled way in the back of the shelf. The less light it has been exposed to, the better for both the oil and your body.

Combining Oils

In almost every dish I invent, I use a combination of oils. For example, I might use one teaspoon of extra virgin olive oil with one teaspoon of almond oil to create a wonderful salad dressing. I encourage you to do the same, and to experiment using your own creativity and ingenuity. **Develop your own personality and blending style - that is the essence of cooking. By experimenting, you will increase your confidence levels and enjoyment in the kitchen.**

My Favorite Extra Virgin Olive Oil

Everyone who produces extra virgin olive oil feels that they unequivocally have the best in the world. Well, if I was producing monkey food, I'd feel that I had the best in the world! The best extra virgin olive oil is the one that you like, and I like California Olive Ranch Extra Virgin Olive Oil.

When it comes to extra virgin olive oil, I want one that ensures freshness throughout the year. I want an extra virgin olive oil that is made like my dinner: to order. Not one that is sitting around and aging like wine.

California Olive Ranch takes advantage of the soil, the climate, the terrain and the sun of our gorgeous 31st state in California. They produce three different varieties of olives to create their products: Arbequina, Arbosana and Koroneiki. They know the groves and the olives the way a mother would know her identical triplets. The consistency of the product relates to its traceability - California Olive Ranch knows right down to the block of land where each olive came from. By identifying codes on each bottle, they let the customers know the olive lineage.

As you are reading through my recipes, you will find that I use extra virgin olive oil on everything from breakfast to dinner, and everything in between. I highly recommend California Olive Ranch because you can smell and taste the freshness in each bottle. A fresh product like this is more likely to contain the polyphenols that provide a real health benefit. Their products are not available everywhere yet, so if you can't find them at your favorite grocery store, check out their online store at **www.californiaoliveranch.com**.

Juicy Information

You will find in my recipes that I try to utilize whole foods. I believe my body deserves the best ingredients I can get my hands on. Therefore, when I look for juice that will benefit my body, I read the ingredient list and see how it was made. Juices that are made from whole organic fruit (not concentrate), and are made without high fructose corn syrup or added sugars are the best for your body.

Here are just a few fruit juices that I love:
• **R.W Knudsen Famiy**
  (Just Concord and Just Black Cherry)

• **Smart Juice**
  (Organic Fig, Apricot, Pomegranate Purple Carrot, and Pomegranate Tart Cherry)

• **Lakewood Organic**
  (Blueberry, Pure Pomegranate, Pure Cranberry, Pure Purple Carrot, Concord Grape)

Alternative milks are easier for your body to digest than regular milks. There are a cornucopia of flavors such as rice, almond, hazelnut, soy, carob and hemp milk. Try to look for those that are made with sunflower or safflower oil, not canola oil. Also, those with minimum amounts of carrageenan (a thickener that you really don't need) are favorable.

Here are just a few brands that I've fallen in love with:
• **All Manitoba Harvest**
  (Hemp Bliss Milk)

• **All Living Harvest** (Hemp Milk)

• **Almond Dream**
  (Original and Unsweetened)

• **Hemp Dream** (Original and Vanilla)

• **EdenSoy** (Original, Vanilla and Carob)

Junk Food

If you like junk food, then go ahead and eat a cupcake or your favorite junk food occasionally and enjoy. Eat and enjoy, then get back on track. Over the long run, it's about what we do every day, not once in a while, that makes the difference.

The Good Fats: Poly and Mono

Polyunsaturated and Monounsaturated fats, unlike saturated fats, are good for you as they aid in the absorption of vitamins A, D, E, and K, and carotenoids. Carotenoids are natural fat-soluble pigments found in plants, algae, and photosynthetic bacteria. Folks who consume foods rich in carotenoids, such as fruits and vegetables, can have lower mortality from a number of chronic illnesses.

You can find polyunsaturated and monounsaturated fats in some fish, seeds, nuts, hemp oil, sunflower oil, safflower oil, extra virgin olive oil, and avocados. These fats offer a host of health benefits and are innocuous when eaten in moderation. You also only need to eat very little of them to get the right amount of nutritive value.

Not-So-Good Fats: Saturated

They taste good, don't they? But saturated fats are considered to be the "not-so-friendly" fats. They can increase heart disease, the leading cause of death in America. We love a lot of things that may have saturated fats in them, so read the label and try not to eat the entire plate or box of treats. Serving size is key!

Very Bad Fats: Trans Fats

Destructive, venomous, and dangerous! These fats are solid fats that are difficult for your body to break down. Before you choose your fats, take a more careful look. If you're going to eat fat, be sure to choose polyunsaturated and monounsaturated fats before trans and saturated fats.

Carbohydrates

Starches and fibers are found in whole grains, cereal, flour, bread, rice, and corn, as well as potatoes, yams, and legumes (i.e. beans, lentils or chickpeas). These are the most efficient form

TONY TIPS

Reading Labels For Fats

How do you read a label that does not provide you with information about polyunsaturated and monounsaturated fats? It's actually easy to decode. Here's the trick: subtract the sum of the trans fats and saturated fats from the "Total Fat" on the label. The remainder is the monounsaturated and polyunsaturated fats!

TONY TIPS

Low Sodium

A food product that is labeled "low sodium" must have 140mg or less on its label. That's important for those watching their sodium intake.

Soluble Fiber is a bulking agent and helps regulate your digestive track. Soluble fiber can help lower cholesterol and regulate blood sugar, which is very advantageous to diabetics and seniors. It is crucial in assisting with our bodily functions. This kind of fiber is found in oat bran, barley, nuts, seeds, flax seed, dried beans, lentils, peas, apple skins, oranges, and carrots. Great for me, great for you, and great for Aunt Sue!

of energy. When you overeat, you store carbohydrates as glycogen for energy. If your body cannot use that energy soon after storing it, then you will eventually wear it as fat.

Both complex carbohydrates (e.g. pasta) and simple carbohydrates (e.g. sugar) are issues for diabetics. Therefore, pasta manufacturers are now using a special fiber called inulin that provides a food source for healthy bacteria living in the stomach. Inulin is a probiotic that promotes digestive health, calcium absorption, and a healthy immune system. It is found naturally in Jerusalem artichokes, sunchokes, asparagus, garlic, and raisins.

Dietary Fiber

Fiber-filled foods are composed of soluble and insoluble fiber. Both types are very important in promoting good health and can reduce some afflictions such as diverticulosis, constipation, and hemorrhoids. So listen up!

While soluble fiber breaks down with liquids; insoluble fiber passes through our intestines largely intact. It adds bulk and resistance to the colon, aids in bacteria balance, controls pH levels in the intestines, and finally, helps with stool elimination. Why am I talking about this? Well, in order for you to be motivated and able to manage your digestion, you first need to understand how it works. Foods like wheat bran, kale, wheatgrass, Swiss chard, and whole grains are great sources of fiber.

TONY TIPS

Take Your Time!

In digesting all of these suggestions, just take your time. You have the rest of your life to eat healthy, so be patient. If you're feeling overwhelmed you should take your time with each step. Enjoy the process. By trying a new healthy behavior each week, you will slowly transition into a healthier lifestyle that you will be able to maintain for years to come. How do you eat an elephant? One bite at a time.

pH 1 – 14
Alkalizing & Acidic Foods

Alkalizing foods are very important! Staying alkalized helps to fight off diseases; infections and viruses are attracted to acidic environments. Over-acidification of the body is a major underlying cause of disease and disorders of the body. Refer to the list on page 19 for examples of acidic and alkalizing foods.

Not Set in Stone

These recipes are not to be confused with the United States Constitution - meaning they are not set in stone. If a recipe calls for an ingredient you cannot find, feel free to substitute it for something else. You have all the freedom in the world; try not to feel imprisoned with the "my way or the highway" approach. Keep in mind, if you change the recipes, chances are, the nutritional facts will changes as well. Therefore, whenever you make ingredient substitutions, the nutritional facts provided with each recipe may no longer be accurate. I encourage you to ask questions when you shop. Most people who work in grocery stores love to talk about groceries. I encourage you to take advantage of that and eat up your free education - it's a great recipe for success!

LINKS
Nutritional & Other Resources

NUTRITIONAL RESOURCES

www.CookingWithTony.com
www.LivingNutritionals.com
www.NavitasNaturals.com
www.ModernFearn.com
www.livingnutritionals.com

OTHER RESOURCES

www.MichaelPolitoPhotography.com
www.AJRoss.com

Appendix A

ALKALINE / ACIDIC FOOD CHARTS

The charts below are provided for those trying to "adjust" their **body pH** through their diet. The pH scale is from **0 to 14**, with numbers below 7 acidic (low on oxygen) and numbers above 7 alkaline. These charts are intended only as a general guide to alkalizing and acidifying foods. Note that there may be some discrepancies between foods included on these charts.*

TABLE OF ACIDIC & ALKALINE
ALKALINE FOODS

ALKALIZING VEGETABLES

Alfalfa	Carrot	Eggplant	Onions
Asparagus	Cauliflower	Fermented Veggies	Parsnips (high glycemic)
Barley Grass	Celery	Garlic	Peas
Beets	Chard Greens	Green Beans	Peppers
Beet Greens	Chlorella	Green Peas	Pumpkin
Broccoli	Collard Greens	Kale	Radishes
Brussels Sprouts	Cucumber	Kohlrabi	Rutabaga
Cabbage	Dandelions	Lettuce	Sauerkraut
	Dulse	Mushrooms	Sea Veggies Baby!
	Edible Flowers	Mustard Greens	

ALKALINE FOODS

Spinach, green
Sprouts
Squash
Spirulina (Blue Green Algae)
Sprouts
Sweet Potatoes
Tomatoes (Ripe)
In deed Watercress
Wheat Grass
Wild Greens

ALKALIZING ORIENTAL VEGETABLES

Maitake
Daikon
Dandelion Root
Shiitake
Kombu
Reishi
Nori
Umeboshi
Wakame

ALKALIZING FRUITS

Apple
Apricot
Avocado
Banana (high glycemic)

Berries
Blackberries
Cantaloupe
Cherries, sour
Coconut, fresh
Citrus Fruit
Currants
Dates, dried
Figs, dried
Grapes
Grapefruit
Honeydew Melon
Lemon
Lime
Melon
Muskmelons
Nectarine
Orange
Peach
Pear
Pineapple
Raisins
Raspberries
Rhubarb
Strawberries
Tangerine
Tomato (Ripe)
Tropical Fruits
Umeboshi Plums
Watermelon

ALKALIZING PROTEIN

Almonds
Chestnuts
Chicken Breast
Cottage Cheese – Fat Free
Eggs
Flaxseed
Millet
Tempeh (fermented)
Tofu (fermented)
Pumpkin Seeds
Squash Seeds
Whey Protein Powder
Yogurt

ALKALIZING SWEETENERS

Stevia

ALKALIZING SPICES & SEASONINGS

Chili Peppers
Cinnamon
Curry
Cayenne Pepper
Ginger
Mustard

Chili Pepper
Sea Salt
Miso
Tamari
All Herbs

ALKALIZING OTHER

Apple Cider Vinegar Raw & Unfiltered
Bee Pollen
Herbal Tea - Tea
Lecithin Granules
Molasses, blackstrap
Probiotic Cultures
Soured Dairy Products
Green Juices
Kombucha
Vegetable Juices
Fresh Fruit Juices
Mineral Water
Alkaline Antioxidant Water

ALKALIZING MINERALS

Cesium: pH 14
Potassium: pH 14
Sodium: pH 14
Calcium: pH 12
Magnesium: pH 9

Although it might seem that citrus fruits would have an acidifying effect on the body, the citric acid they contain actually has **alkalinizing properties**. Lemons and Apple Cider Vinegar are good examples.

You don't need to adhere strictly to the Alkaline diet, just make sure a good percentage of the foods you eat come from that alkaline side.

ACIDIC FOODS

ACIDIFYING VEGETABLES

Corn
Lentils
Winter Squash
Potatoes (white)

ACIDIFYING FRUITS

Blueberries
Canned or Glazed
Fruits
Cranberries
Currants
Plums**
Prunes**
Olives

ACIDIFYING GRAINS, GRAIN PRODUCTS

Amaranth
Barley
Bran, wheat
Bran, oat
Buckwheat
Corn
Cornstarch
Hemp Seed Flour
Kamut
Oats (rolled)
Oatmeal
Quinoa
Rice (all)
Rice Cakes
Rye
Spelt
Wheat
Wheat Germ
Noodles
Macaroni
Spaghetti
Bread

Crackers, soda
Flour, white
Flour, wheat

ACIDIFYING BEANS & LEGUMES

Black Beans
Chick Peas
Green Peas
Kidney Beans
Lentils
Lima Beans
Pinto Beans
Pinto Beans
Potato
Red Beans
Soy Beans
Soy Milk
White Beans
Rice Milk
Almond Milk

ACIDIFYING DAIRY

Butter
Cheese
Cheese, Processed
Ice Cream
Ice Milk
Milk

ACIDIFYING NUTS & BUTTERS

Brazil
Cashews
Filbert
Legumes
Peanuts
Peanut Butter
Pecans
Tahini
Walnuts

ACIDIFYING ANIMAL PROTEIN

Bacon
Beef
Carp
Clams
Cod
Corned Beef
Duck
Fish
Haddock
Lamb
Lobster
Mussels
Organ Meats
Oyster
Pike
Pork
Rabbit
Salmon
Sardines
Sausage
Scallops
Shrimp
Scallops
Shellfish
Tuna
Turkey
Veal
Venison

ACIDIFYING FATS & OILS

Avacado Oil
Butter
Canola Oil
Corn Oil
Hemp Seed Oil
Flax Oil
Lard
Olive Oil
Safflower Oil

Sesame Oil
Sunflower Oil

ACIDIFYING SWEETENERS

Aspartame
Corn Syrup
Carob
Honey (Manuka)
Saccharin
Sugar

ACIDIFYING ALCOHOL

Beer
Spirits
Hard Liquor / Spirits
Wine

ACIDIFYING OTHER FOODS

Catsup
Cocoa
Coffee
Vinegar
Mustard
Pepper
Soft Drinks

ACIDIFYING DRUGS & CHEMICALS

Aspirin
Chemicals
Drugs
Pesticides
Herbicides
Tobacco

ACIDIFYING JUNK FOOD

Coca-Cola: pH 2
Beer: pH 2.5
Coffee: pH 4

** These foods leave an alkaline ash but have an acidifying effect on the body.

These statements have not been evaluated by the Food and Drug Administration and are not intended to diagnose, treat, cure, or prevent any disease; research is ongoing.

http://www.essense-of-life.com/moreinfo/foodcharts.htm

BREAKFAST

AVOCADO OMELET WITH PEA SPROUTS

CRUNCHY ALMOND BUTTER SNACK

RUBY RED GRAPEFRUIT & PEAR WITH GINGER SAUCE

TOASTY, SWEET ONION EGG WHITE SANDWICH

8 Minutes

AVOCADO OMELET WITH PEA SPROUTS

SERVES 2

1) 2 tsp Sunflower Oil
2) 1 Small Onion (thinly sliced on mandolin)
3) 3 Egg Whites
4) 1 Egg Yolk
5) Pinch of Cayenne Pepper
6) Spike Seasoning, to taste
7) 1 Clove of Garlic (minced)
8) ½ Avocado (sliced)
9) 2 TBSP Pea Sprouts
10) ½ tsp Chives (chopped)

In a hot skillet, heat sunflower oil and sauté onion for one minute. In a bowl, whisk together ingredients 3–7 with your spatula. Pour mixture into skillet and cook for two minutes. Place thinly sliced avocado on half of the circle formed in the pan by the egg mixture. Then, add pea sprouts and fold egg in half to make the omelet. Cook for an additional two minutes and finish by topping with chopped chives.

To make it dance ~ Drizzle with extra virgin olive oil and the juice and zest of ¼ lemon. If you like nut flavored oil, go ahead and try walnut, almond or hazelnut oil. Cilantro is always a nice finish, as is a touch of crème fraîche.

Nutrition Facts

Serv. Size 4 oz (113g)

Calories 170

Fat Cal. 120

Amount/serving	%DV*	Amount/serving	%DV*
Total Fat 14g	21%	Total Carb. 6g	2%
Sat. Fat 2.5g	13%	Fiber 4g	14%
Trans Fat 0g		Sugars 2g	
Cholest. 115mg	38%	Protein 7g	
Sodium 65mg	3%		

*Percent Daily Values (DV) are based on a 2,000 calorie diet.

Vitamin A 6% • Vitamin C 20% • Calcium 2% • Iron 2%

CRUNCHY ALMOND BUTTER SNACK

SERVES 1

1) 2 TBSP of Crunchy Almond Butter
2) 1 Slice Whole Grain Bread (my favorite is Mestemacher)

This is a filling and healthy morning snack. Almond butter is higher in fiber, iron, and vitamins and lower in fat than peanut butter. Simply spread almond butter over bread. Slice the bread in half and enjoy. This pairs wonderfully with a cup of your favorite tea. Just one recommendation - eat this slowly.

To make it lighter ~ If you prefer, try it with a plain (no-sugar) rice cake. There are an unlimited amount of choices for rice cakes, but be sure to read the ingredient list to check the sugar content.

Nutrition Facts	Amount/serving	%DV*	Amount/serving	%DV*
Serv. Size 2 oz (57g)	Total Fat 15g	23%	Total Carb. 22g	7%
	Sat. Fat 1.5g	8%	Fiber 3g	12%
Calories 240	Trans Fat 0g		Sugars 4g	
Fat Cal. 130	Cholest. 0mg	0%	Protein 7g	
	Sodium 180mg	8%		
*Percent Daily Values (DV) are based on a 2,000 calorie diet.	Vitamin A 0% • Vitamin C 0%		• Calcium 10% • Iron 10%	

2 Minutes

RUBY RED GRAPEFRUIT & PEAR WITH GINGER SAUCE

SERVES 2

1) 1 Ruby Red Grapefruit
2) 1 Ripe Pear
3) 1 tsp Ginger (minced)
4) ½ tsp Rapadura (real sugar cane)
5) 1 Orange (zest)

This is a juicy breakfast or dessert recipe. Peel grapefruit and pear. Then, juice half the grapefruit and reserve. Cut the pear and the other half of grapefruit into quarters. Toss them in a bowl with minced ginger and rapadura. Ginger can be bought already minced, or if whole, you can shave the ginger root with a spoon (not with a peeler) - all you need is about a ¼-inch piece. Lastly, pour reserved grapefruit juice into the bowl. To garnish, slice the orange peel into matchsticks and place on top of your dish.

To give it a twist ~ Add 4 oz. of papaya juice or shaved bittersweet chocolate to the mix. For a better, healthier choice, toss some cacao (sweetened) nibs on top - you'll love it!

Nutrition Facts	Amount/serving	%DV*	Amount/serving	%DV*
Serv. Size 6 oz (170g)	Total Fat 0g	0%	Total Carb. 20g	7%
	Sat. Fat 0g	0%	Fiber 2g	9%
Calories 80	Trans Fat 0g		Sugars 7g	
Fat Cal. 0	Cholest. 0mg	0%	Protein 1g	
	Sodium 0mg	0%		
*Percent Daily Values (DV) are based on a 2,000 calorie diet.	Vitamin A 8% • Vitamin C 70% • Calcium 2% • Iron 2%			

TOASTY, SWEET ONION EGG WHITE SANDWICH

SERVES 1

1) 1 TBSP Sunflower Oil
2) 1 Clove of Garlic (diced)
3) ½ Small Onion (thinly sliced)
4) 1 Egg White
5) 2 Mint Leaves (finely chopped)
6) Salt and Pepper, to taste
7) Dash of Cayenne Pepper
8) 1 Whole Wheat English Muffin or Unbleached Breakfast Roll

In a hot skillet, heat the sunflower oil. Add ingredients 2 and 3 and sauté for three to four minutes. Add ingredients 4–7 to skillet and cook for an additional two minutes. During this time, using your spatula, form an egg patty in the shape of your breakfast roll. Remove patty and set aside on plate. Slice breakfast roll in half. Add another drop of sunflower oil to the now empty skillet and toast your breakfast roll until golden brown. Place egg patty inside of roll, slice in half and serve.

To make it soy-licious ~ Try scrambled tofu in place of the egg. Also, try replacing mint leaves with clove powder. Cloves have a strong earthy and aromatic taste to them. You could also spread 1 tsp of crème fraîche on the roll prior to adding the egg - it's a great complement.

Nutrition Facts

Serv. Size 6 oz (170g)

Calories 220

Fat Cal. 50

Amount/serving	%DV*	Amount/serving	%DV*
Total Fat 5g	8%	Total Carb. 34g	11%
Sat. Fat 1.5g	7%	Fiber 2g	9%
Trans Fat 0g		Sugars 3g	
Cholest. 0mg	0%	Protein 8g	
Sodium 125mg	5%		

*Percent Daily Values (DV) are based on a 2,000 calorie diet.

Vitamin A 10% • Vitamin C 10% • Calcium 10% • Iron 20%

10 Minutes

SHAKES

BANANA AND BLUEBERRY SHAKE

BANANA AND STRAWBERRY SHAKE WITH CACAO NIBS

PASSIONATE MANGO SMOOTHIE

STRAWBERRY SHAKE

6 Minutes

BANANA AND BLUEBERRY SHAKE

SERVES ABOUT 3

1) 3 Bananas
2) ¾ C. Concord Grape Juice (R.W. KnudsenFamily is my favorite)
3) ¾ C. Almond Milk
4) ¼ C. Blueberries
5) 1 TBSP Hemp Oil
6) Dash of Cayenne pepper
7) Dash of Cinnamon
8) 4 Ice Cubes
9) 1 TBSP Lemon Juice

Combine ingredients 1-4 in a food processor/blender. Pulse four to five times. Once incorporated, add ingredients 5-7. You could also add 1 TBSP of probiotic powder (Green Vibrance is my favorite). Continue to blend well. Lastly, add the ice cubes and lemon juice to the food processor/blender and pulse until fully crushed. Enjoy this cool, fresh and nutritious shake! Don't forget – the body loves liquids because it's very little work to digest.

If this shake is too thick, just add more liquid. By choosing different liquids such as hazelnut milk, rice milk, or carob soy milk, you change the flavor and can keep the shake interesting.

Eat this ~ "Pro" means "for" or "in favor of" and "biotic" means "life." Therefore, probiotic means "for or in favor of life." With that said, "anti" means "against." Therefore, antibiotic means "not in favor of life," essentially "killing life." Give live, friendly bacteria and probiotics to your body. It will help restore, promote and maintain your health as you age.

Nutrition Facts	Amount/serving	%DV*	Amount/serving	%DV*
Serv. Size 9 oz (255g)	**Total Fat** 1.5g	2%	**Total Carb.** 43g	14%
Calories 190	Sat. Fat 0g	0%	Fiber 8g	31%
Fat Cal. 10	*Trans* Fat 0g		Sugars 19g	
	Cholest. 0mg	0%	**Protein** 5g	
	Sodium 5mg	0%		
*Percent Daily Values (DV) are based on a 2,000 calorie diet.	Vitamin A 8% • Vitamin C 50% • Calcium 2% • Iron 4%			

BANANA AND STRAWBERRY SHAKE WITH CACAO NIBS

SERVES 3

1) 3 Bananas
2) 1 C. Carob Soy Milk (or any juice)
3) 5 Strawberries (cut off green ends)
4) 1/4 Lemon (cut into smaller quarters without removing skin)
5) 1 Clove of Garlic
6) 1 TBSP Hemp Oil
7) 4 Ice Cubes
8) 8 Cacao Beans or a Handful Cacao Nibs

Combine ingredients 1 and 2 in food processor/blender and pulse for five seconds. Once ingredients are incorporated, turn to high speed. Add ingredients 3-5 and blend for ten more seconds. Add ingredients 6-8 and blend for 30 seconds. There are many variations to this. Try to make your own - it's really hard to mess this up!

Many of you are thinking "Garlic? Is this guy out of his tree?". Believe me – I haven't steered you wrong – the garlic is subtle in this shake. It's not a must-have ingredient, but it's a great addition. If you like, garnish with orange peel or a strawberry. If you like more liquidity, add more juice, rice milk, almond milk or a little soy milk. You can always add more liquid if it is too thick.

Eat this ~ Choosing different liquids (such as almond milk, rice milk or grape juice) can give the shakes variety and help to mix things up to keep you satisfied. By drinking it slowly, your body will have a chance to fully digest. Since it's liquid, the body won't need to work as hard to break the food down. Also, remember to read the labels on the back of any fruit juice you buy. You want to make sure that the juice was made from ripe, whole certified organic strawberries, blueberries, and blackberries or apple cider.

Nutrition Facts

Serv. Size 9 oz (255g)

Calories 190

Fat Cal. 35

Amount/serving	%DV*	Amount/serving	%DV*
Total Fat 4g	6%	Total Carb. 39g	13%
Sat. Fat 2g	11%	Fiber 7g	26%
Trans Fat 0g		Sugars 18g	
Cholest. 5mg	1%	Protein 4g	
Sodium 25mg	1%		

*Percent Daily Values (DV) are based on a 2,000 calorie diet.

Vitamin A 2% • Vitamin C 70% • Calcium 6% • Iron 6%

6 Minutes

7 Minutes

PASSIONATE MANGO SMOOTHIE

SERVES ABOUT 1 ½

1) 1 Ripe Mango
2) 1 Passion Fruit
3) 4 Ice Cubes
4) Dash of Cinnamon
5) Dash of Cayenne Pepper
6) ½ C. Apricot Juice

Remove skin and stone from the mango – this should take about three minutes. Once completed, slice passion fruit in half and remove all the "meat" from the inside. No folks, I don't mean for you to add ground beef or pork! I mean you should remove all that you can from the inside of the fruit. Combine all ingredients in a food processor and pulse for ten seconds or until all ingredients are blended. If desired, you can replace apricot juice with grape, cherry or lime juice.

Eat this ~ Apricots are full of beta-carotene and fiber and have a decent amount of vitamin C. They are great as a topping for sherbet or you can eat them dried, diced or shaved. I would say the flavor is musky and pungent, with a hint of tartness.

Nutrition Facts	Amount/serving	%DV*	Amount/serving	%DV*
Serv. Size 6 oz (170g)	Total Fat 0g	0%	Total Carb. 21g	7%
	Sat. Fat 0g	0%	Fiber 1g	6%
Calories 80	Trans Fat 0g		Sugars 19g	
Fat Cal. 0	Cholest. 0mg	0%	Protein 1g	
	Sodium 0mg	0%		
*Percent Daily Values (DV) are based on a 2,000 calorie diet.	Vitamin A 15% • Vitamin C 60% • Calcium 2% • Iron 2%			

STRAWBERRY SHAKE

SERVES ABOUT 2

1) 12 Strawberries
2) ½ C. Grape Juice (R.W. Knudsen Family is my favorite)
3) ½ C. Almond Milk
4) 1 TBSP Hemp Powder or Probiotic Powder (Green Vibrance is my favorite)
5) 3 Ice Cubes
6) 3 Shakes of Nutmeg

Combine all ingredients in food processor/blender. Pulse four to five times before reverting to high speed. Remember to drink this slowly. This is your chance to add anything you want to this shake, but you should add everything slowly, and in small increments. As an alternative to almond milk, try pomegranate juice or your favorite fruit juice.

Remember to read the ingredients on juice; try not to buy any that are from concentrate.

Nutrition Facts	Amount/serving	%DV*	Amount/serving	%DV*
Serv. Size 9 oz (255g)	**Total Fat** 4.5g	7%	**Total Carb.** 23g	8%
Calories 140	Sat. Fat 2g	10%	Fiber 7g	30%
Fat Cal. 40	Trans Fat 0g		Sugars 13g	
	Cholest. 0mg	0%	**Protein** 4g	
	Sodium 40mg	2%		
*Percent Daily Values (DV) are based on a 2,000 calorie diet.	Vitamin A 0% •	Vitamin C 110% •	Calcium 4% •	Iron 6%

4
Minutes

SOUPS

CHUNKY TOMATO SOUP

FRESH AND SIMPLE CANNELLINI BEAN SOUP

NOT-SO-CLASSIC MINESTRONE SOUP

STRAWBERRY SUMMER SOUP

10 Minutes

CHUNKY TOMATO SOUP

SERVES ABOUT 2

1) 1 TBSP Sunflower Oil
2) ½ Spanish Onion (thinly sliced on mandolin)
3) 1 Clove of Garlic (minced)
4) ¼ C. Edamame
5) ½ C. Chicken Stock
6) Salt and Pepper, to taste
7) 1 can Chunky Tomato Bisque (I like Amy's Organic Soups)
8) ¼ Lemon (juice)
9) Basil or Parsley, to garnish

Heat sunflower oil in a pot or skillet and combine ingredients 2-6. Cook for three to five minutes. Add canned soup and cook for two more minutes. Lastly, add lemon and basil or parsley for garnish.

Try this recipe with a variety of soups. Some, like lentil or beef, are hearty so the spices that you add might change. Some of my favorite spices for richer soups are coriander, cumin and curry powder. All you need is a little ingenuity and creativity!

For a fiesta in your mouth ~ Garnish with chunks of avocado and cilantro.

Nutrition Facts Serv. Size 6 oz (170g)	Amount/serving	%DV*	Amount/serving	%DV*
Calories 110	**Total Fat** 6g	9%	**Total Carb.** 10g	3%
Fat Cal. 50	Sat. Fat 0.5g	3%	Fiber 2g	9%
	Trans Fat 0g		Sugars 4g	
	Cholest. 0mg	0%	**Protein** 6g	
	Sodium 45mg	2%		
*Percent Daily Values (DV) are based on a 2,000 calorie diet.	Vitamin A 8% • Vitamin C 45% • Calcium 8% • Iron 10%			

FRESH AND SIMPLE CANNELLINI BEAN SOUP

SERVES ABOUT 1 ½

1) 1 TBSP Sunflower Oil
2) 2 Cloves of Garlic (minced)
3) 1 C. Cannellini Beans (drained)
4) Dash of Sea Seasoning
5) ½ C. Vegetable Broth
6) Fresh Pepper, to taste
7) 1 TBSP Parsley (finely chopped)
8) ¼ Lemon (juice and zest)
9) 1 tsp Basil (chopped)

Heat sunflower oil in skillet and combine ingredients 2–7. Cook for seven minutes. Remove, let cool for a minute, and then pulse in your food processor for five seconds.

If you decide not to puree it, I'd recommend using less liquid and this soup can turn into a beautiful and easy side dish. Use your imagination and try some of the alternatives to cannellini beans, such as soy beans, black beans, peas, kidney beans, or chickpeas (garbanzo beans). You can replace the broth with canned tomato sauce or chicken/beef stock. Soups are endless with possibility!

To add some heat ~ I'll always hit it with a touch of cayenne pepper or curry powder. While you're at it, add pistachio nuts for a nice, crunchy finish.

Nutrition Facts	Amount/serving	%DV*	Amount/serving	%DV*
Serv. Size 7 oz (198g)	Total Fat 11g	17%	Total Carb. 15g	5%
Calories 170	Sat. Fat 1.5g	7%	Fiber 1g	5%
Fat Cal. 100	*Trans* Fat 0g		Sugars 0g	
	Cholest. 0mg	0%	Protein 9g	
	Sodium 340mg	14%		
*Percent Daily Values (DV) are based on a 2,000 calorie diet.	Vitamin A 10% • Vitamin C 90% • Calcium 15% • Iron 25%			

9 Minutes

10 Minutes

NOT-SO-CLASSIC MINESTRONE SOUP

SERVES ABOUT 1

1) 1 TBSP Sunflower Oil
2) ½ Spanish Onion (finely chopped)
3) 1 Clove of Garlic (minced)
4) 1 Celery Stalk (finely chopped)
5) ⅓ C. Vegetable Broth
6) ⅓ C. Fresh Ziti (sliced into small "Cherrios")
7) 4 Plum Tomatoes
8) 1 TBSP Parsley (finely chopped)
9) Salt and Pepper to taste

Heat sunflower oil in skillet and combine ingredients 2–4. Cook for three minutes, then add ingredients 5-7 and cook for two more minutes. Combine ingredients 7-9 in your food processor and pulse for 6 to 8 seconds. Remove, add to skillet and lower heat. Cook for an additional minute or until soup is warm to your lips. Finally, add parsley to garnish. To speed this up replace the tomatoes with 5 oz. of your favorite tomato sauce.

To put muscles on it ~ Add a handful of baby spinach in skillet to wilt or garnish on top.

Eat this ~ The pasta that's actually used in the classic minestrone is ditalini, which means "little thimbles" in Italian. You can easily use other types of fresh pasta, like a simple tortellini. If you desire a healthier choice, go with gluten-free pasta.

Note: Celery makes up 23mg of sodium in this recipe.

Nutrition Facts Serv. Size 7 oz (198g)	Amount/serving	%DV*	Amount/serving	%DV*
	Total Fat 7g	**11%**	**Total Carb.** 22g	**7%**
	Sat. Fat 0.5g	**4%**	Fiber 2g	**9%**
Calories 170	*Trans* Fat 0g		Sugars 4g	
Fat Cal. 60	**Cholest.** 20mg	**6%**	**Protein** 5g	
	Sodium 140mg	**6%**		
*Percent Daily Values (DV) are based on a 2,000 calorie diet.	Vitamin A 50% • Vitamin C 30% • Calcium 6% • Iron 10%			

STRAWBERRY SUMMER SOUP

SERVES ABOUT 2

1) 3 C. Fresh Strawberries
2) 1 C. Vanilla Yogurt Fat-free
3) 1 Fresh Vanilla Bean (remove from vanilla seed)
4) ¼ Lemon (juice)
5) ¼ C. Orange Juice
6) Dash of Clove Powder
7) ½ tsp Cinnamon
8) 1 tsp Manuka Honey or Agave Nectar
9) 1 tsp Crème Fraîche, to garnish (optional)
10) ¼ C. Dried Blueberries (optional)

Get ready for a delicious soup, served cold or warm. In your food processor, place ingredients 1–8 and puree for eight seconds. Don't bother removing the stems from the strawberries. Once incorporated in the food processor, remove and strain, using a sieve and a spatula to push the juice through into a pot. Once all of the liquid is in the pot, add 1 tsp of the pulp from the sieve and stir it into the soup. If you prefer this soup cold, serve immediately. If you like it hot, simply heat on low for three minutes. To plate: give yourself a dollop of crème fraîche in the center and garnish with fresh or dried berries. Treat yourself to this delicious mid-morning snack, afternoon treat or appetizer.

To make this fresh ~ Roll partially frozen cream cheese into small pea-sized balls as a topping. You probably only need about 4-6 balls. Another option is to drizzle heavy cream, cacao powder or pistachio nuts over the top.

Eat This ~ Agave Nectar is derived from the same plant from which tequila is born. A product of Mexico, the given name is agumiel. Agave Nectar is a natural sweetener that won't make your blood sugar levels spike because it has a low-glycemic index (GI).

Nutrition Facts	Amount/serving	%DV*	Amount/serving	%DV*
Serv. Size 7 oz (198g)	Total Fat 0.5g	1%	Total Carb. 17g	6%
	Sat. Fat 0g	0%	Fiber 4g	15%
Calories 80	Trans Fat 0g		Sugars 12g	
Fat Cal. 5	Cholest. 0mg	0%	Protein 3g	
	Sodium 30mg	1%		
*Percent Daily Values (DV) are based on a 2,000 calorie diet.	Vitamin A 0% • Vitamin C 150% • Calcium 10% • Iron 8%			

9 Minutes

SALADS

BABY SPINACH WITH AVOCADO AND CHICKPEAS

BUTTERNUT SQUASH WITH BABY ROMAINE LETTUCE

CRISPY SALAD WITH LEMON PEPPER DRESSING

FIELD GREENS WITH BURDOCK ROOT AND GOAT CHEESE

MINTY RED CABBAGE SALAD

MISO HUNGRY DRESSING

NUTTY SPRING SALAD WITH LEMON AND LIME DRESSING

SWEET DANDELION SALAD WITH SPROUTS

TANGY DIJON MUSTARD SALAD

10 Minutes

BABY SPINACH WITH AVOCADO AND TERMIS BEANS

SERVES 4

Salad:
1) 1 Bag Baby Spinach
2) 6 oz. Temis Beans (Chickpeas Optional)
3) 1 Avocado (remove stone and slice thinly)
4) 1/4 C. Sliced Almonds (unsalted)
5) Pinch of Salt

Dressing:
6) 1 Lemon (juice and zest)
7) 3 TBSP Extra Virgin Olive Oil
8) 1 TBSP Balsamic Vinegar (preferably Villa Manodori)
9) 1 tsp Sour Cream
10) 1 tsp Chives (chopped)
11) Dash of Cayenne Pepper
12) Fresh Black Pepper, to taste

For the Salad:
Combine ingredients in a bowl and mix well.

For the Dressing:
Combine ingredients in a bowl and toss softly. Then combine salad mixture with dressing and fold together. If the salad seems a little dry, drizzle extra virgin olive oil over it until it shines.

Eat this ~ Cayenne pepper is a natural pain reliever. It can help clear congestion and boost immunity. It also has cardiovascular benefits and can prevent stomach ulcers. Cayenne pepper is packed with vitamin A and is a good source of other vitamins like B6, C and K. Try getting cayenne pepper at grocery stores that have a wide selection of dried herbs that are fresh.

Nutrition Facts

Serv. Size 4 oz (113g)
Calories 230
Fat Cal. 80

Amount/serving	%DV*	Amount/serving	%DV*
Total Fat 9g	15%	Total Carb. 27g	9%
Sat. Fat 1g	5%	Fiber 4g	17%
Trans Fat 0g		Sugars 1g	
Cholest. 0mg	0%	Protein 11g	
Sodium 60mg	2%		

*Percent Daily Values (DV) are based on a 2,000 calorie diet.

Vitamin A 110% • Vitamin C 30% • Calcium 10% • Iron 25%

SERVES ABOUT 3

1) ½ C. Butternut Squash (peeled and cubed)
2) 1 Clove of Garlic (diced)
3) 1 Bag Romaine Lettuce
4) 2 TBSP Extra Virgin Olive Oil
5) 1 tsp Dill (finely minced)
7) 1 tsp Chickpea Miso (South River Miso is my favorite)
8) Dash of Seasoning (try Borsari brand)
9) ½ Lemon (juice and zest)
10) Handful Cherry Tomatoes (cut in half)

In your food processor, combine squash and garlic and pulse for four to seven seconds. Remove and place in large bowl with romaine lettuce and mix well. In a smaller bowl, combine ingredients 4–8 and whisk well. Combine dressing with lettuce and toss. To finish, add ingredients 9 and 10.

To make it dance ~ Add a few nuts. I love cashews, pistachios, or sliced almonds. They introduce character to this dish, not to mention vitamin E! Whatever can fit in your hand is a fair amount. Remember "if it fits, it ships". I like my salad to shine by drizzling 1 tsp of almond oil, hazelnut oil or hemp oil over them.

Nutrition Facts	Amount/serving	%DV*	Amount/serving	%DV*
Serv. Size 3 oz (85g)	Total Fat 0.5g	1%	Total Carb. 6g	2%
	Sat. Fat 0g	0%	Fiber 1g	6%
Calories 30	Trans Fat 0g		Sugars 1g	
Fat Cal. 0	Cholest. 0mg	0%	Protein 1g	
	Sodium 65mg	3%		
*Percent Daily Values (DV) are based on a 2,000 calorie diet.	Vitamin A 90% • Vitamin C 25% • Calcium 2% • Iron 4%			

10 Minutes

10 Minutes

CRISPY SALAD WITH LEMON PEPPER DRESSING

SERVES 5

Salad:
1) ¼ C. Jicama
2) ½ C. Fennel
3) Handful of Cilantro (roughly chopped)
4) ¼ C. Frozen Corn or Sweet Corn
5) 8 Snow Pea Pods
6) 10 Cashews (crushed)

Dressing:
7) 2 TBSP Extra Virgin Olive Oil
8) Pepper, to taste
9) 1 TBSP Almond Oil
10) ½ Lemon (zest and juice)

For the Salad:
With your knife or mandolin, shave the layer of skin from the jicama. Slice it into about ten disks on mandolin. Then, slice into matchsticks and place into bowl. Chop up fennel (including the ferns) and combine with cilantro and corn. Toss all ingredients together. Lastly, add ingredients 5 and 6 to bowl. Toss well.

For the Dressing:
In a bowl, whisk all ingredients and drizzle over salad.

To make this crunchy ~ Add a few crushed corn chips. An elegant twist to this dish would be grilled asparagus cut into quarters and seasoned with sea salt. Kick off your shoes and sink your teeth into a juicy lunch, snack or dinner.

Nutrition Facts	Amount/serving	%DV*	Amount/serving	%DV*
Serv. Size 5 oz (142g)	Total Fat 7g	11%	Total Carb. 24g	8%
	Sat. Fat 1g	4%	Fiber 9g	34%
Calories 170	Trans Fat 0g		Sugars 2g	
Fat Cal. 60	Cholest. 0mg	0%	Protein 10g	
	Sodium 150mg	6%		
*Percent Daily Values (DV) are based on a 2,000 calorie diet.	Vitamin A 2% • Vitamin C 80% • Calcium 25% • Iron 60%			

SERVES ABOUT 3

Salad:
1) 1 Bag of Mixed Field Greens
2) 1 Raw Red Beet (sliced)
3) 1 Burdock Root or Carrots
4) 1 C. Crumbled Goat Cheese
5) ¼ Lemon (juice and zest)

Dressing:
6) 1 TBSP Extra Virgin Olive Oil
7) 1 tsp Villa Manodori Balsamic Vinegar or Apple Cider Vinegar
8) Fresh Black Pepper and Sea Salt, to taste
9) 2 Shakes of Cayenne Pepper
10) ½ tsp Honey Mustard

For the Salad:

On your mandolin, slice the beet, creating six thin disks. Shred the burdock root on your grater. I know you are probably thinking, "Burdock root? Are you kidding me?". Wait a second before you go running out of the kitchen! This is one vegetable that you cannot judge until you try it; it's nutty and sweet. Toss ingredients 1-3 in a bowl. Garnish with lemon and juice.

For the Dressing:

In a bowl, combine ingredients 6-10 and whisk together. You can also use Spike Seasonings. They are great alternatives to salt. Look for these at your Whole Foods Market or at your favorite grocery store.

To make this memorable ~ Crush or chop 6 Kalamata olives with a handful of corn chips and lay them in a whole wheat, gluten-free or tortilla pita. Then add a handful of the mixture above. Roll it up tight and sink your teeth in! If mache lettuce is in season, I highly recommend trying it in place of the mixed field greens. It is a soft and delicate lettuce that grows in small clusters.

Nutrition Facts	Amount/serving	%DV*	Amount/serving	%DV*
Serv. Size 4 oz (113g)	Total Fat 9g	15%	Total Carb. 4g	1%
Calories 120	Sat. Fat 3.5g	18%	Fiber 6g	24%
Fat Cal. 80	Trans Fat 0g		Sugars 2g	
	Cholest. 10mg	3%	Protein 6g	
	Sodium 160mg	7%		
*Percent Daily Values (DV) are based on a 2,000 calorie diet.	Vitamin A 140% • Vitamin C 30% • Calcium 8% • Iron 25%			

10 Minutes

7 Minutes

MINTY RED CABBAGE SALAD

SERVES 4

1) ¼ of a Red Cabbage
2) ¼ Lemon (juice and zest)
3) 3 Mint Leaves
4) 1 Clove of Garlic
5) 1 tsp Chickpea Miso
6) 1 tsp Mayonnaise
7) 2 TBSP Extra Virgin Olive Oil
8) Splash of Apple Cider Vinegar (Braggs is my favorite)
9) 3 C. Baby Spinach
10) ¼ C. Buckwheat

In a food processor, combine ingredients 1–4 and pulse four to six times – about six seconds each time. Remove and place on reserve. In a bowl, combine ingredients 5–8 and whisk well. Add ingredients 9 and 10 to bowl. Toss in reserved ingredients and serve.

You can replace the mint with cilantro or basil. If you don't like one of the ingredients, feel free to omit it. Adding meat will also taste great, but don't forget - it will increase the fat content.

Eat this ~ Buckwheat is loaded with magnesium which helps relax blood vessels and aids in lowering blood pressure, yet increasing blood flow - a superb combination for a healthy cardiovascular system. How do you like that, Spanky?

Nutrition Facts	Amount/serving	%DV*	Amount/serving	%DV*
Serv. Size 4 oz (113g)	Total Fat 6g	9%	Total Carb. 14g	5%
	Sat. Fat 1g	4%	Fiber 6g	22%
Calories 120	Trans Fat 0g		Sugars 2g	
Fat Cal. 50	Cholest. 0mg	0%	Protein 4g	
	Sodium 100mg	4%		
*Percent Daily Values (DV) are based on a 2,000 calorie diet.	Vitamin A 2% • Vitamin C 40% • Calcium 6% • Iron 20%			

SERVES 4

1) 1 tsp Chickpea Miso (South River Miso is my top choice)
2) 2 TBSP Extra Virgin Olive Oil
3) 1 tsp Villa Manodori Balsamic Vinegar or Apple Cider Vinegar
4) 2 Shakes of Curry Powder
5) Pepper, to taste
6) 1 tsp Almond Oil
7) ¼ Lemon (juice)

In a bowl, combine all ingredients and mix. This is great for dressing up grilled fish, chicken or asparagus. Mix any herbaceous greens with this dressing. I love it with dandelions or with baby arugula and sweet corn. Miso already has salt, so there is no need to add more.

To make it sassy ~ Add 1 tsp mayonnaise and 4 drops of white truffle oil - you'll change the entire dish. Again, with just a few different oils, you will have a completely different salad dressing. Trying new things and being creative with these recipes will help build confidence when you cook. Someone special will love enjoying this dressing with you!

Nutrition Facts	Amount/serving	%DV*	Amount/serving	%DV*
Serv. Size 1 oz (28g)	Total Fat 13g	20%	Total Carb. 2g	1%
	Sat. Fat 1.5g	8%	Fiber 1g	3%
Calories 120	*Trans* Fat 0g		Sugars 0g	
Fat Cal. 110	**Cholest.** 0mg	0%	**Protein** 1g	
	Sodium 150mg	6%		
*Percent Daily Values (DV) are based on a 2,000 calorie diet.	Vitamin A 0%	• Vitamin C 15%	• Calcium 2%	• Iron 2%

4
Minutes

10 Minutes

SERVES 4

Salad:

1) 1 Bag Spring Mix Salad
2) 1 Plum Tomato (diced)
3) 1 TBSP Parsley (diced)
4) $\frac{1}{3}$ C. Avocado (diced - 3g of good fat!)
5) 1 Bag Raw Termis Beans (about 6 ounces)

Dressing:

6) 3 TBSP Extra Virgin Olive Oil
7) $\frac{1}{2}$ Lemon (juice and zest)
8) 1 Lime (juice)
9) $\frac{1}{2}$ tsp Ginger (peeled and minced)
10) $\frac{1}{2}$ tsp Kelp Seasoning

For the Salad:

Termis beans are delicious nutty flavored beans. If you have a hard time finding termis beans, you can use chickpeas (garbanzo beans.) Combine all ingredients and toss well.

For the Dressing:

In a bowl, combine all ingredients and whisk well. Then top over salad.

To make this cheesy ~ Try Wisconsin's Antigo Stravecchio Parmesan Cheese, it's half the cost of Parmigiano Reggiano and has a fairly similar taste. Capers would also be a great addition to the dish and lends itself well to the cheese flavor.

Nutrition Facts	Amount/serving	%DV*	Amount/serving	%DV*
Serv. Size 5 oz (142g)	Total Fat 4g	6%	Total Carb. 5g	2%
	Sat. Fat 0.5g	3%	Fiber 8g	30%
Calories 60	Trans Fat 0g		Sugars 1g	
Fat Cal. 35	Cholest. 0mg	0%	Protein 3g	
	Sodium 80mg	3%		
*Percent Daily Values (DV) are based on a 2,000 calorie diet.	Vitamin A 6% • Vitamin C 35% • Calcium 6% • Iron 30%			

SWEET DANDELION SALAD WITH SPROUTS

SERVES ABOUT 3

1) 1 TBSP Extra Virgin Olive Oil
2) 1 tsp Manuka Honey
3) ¼ Lemon (juice)
4) Dash of Sea Salt
5) Handful of Dandelion Greens (or any leafy vegetable)
6) ¼ C. Sprouted Mung and Adzuki Beans

In a bowl, combine ingredients 1-4 and whisk well. Then, incorporate dandelion greens and sprouts. If you are unable to find dandelion greens, feel free to use any leafy vegetable instead.

To make it vibrant ~ Adding color to your salads can be fun and delicious; Oranges, dried blueberries or pomegranate seeds are a nice addition. If you like nuts, try cashews, hazelnuts or almonds; they are packed with vitamin E and are a great source of the good fats. The nuts will change the nutritional facts, but they will add a nice crunch. Just remember: what fits in your hand is more than enough for a serving.

Eat this ~ Manuka honey is quite different from the traditional honey that we know today. Manuka is the best honey - it is an antiseptic, antiviral, antioxidant, anti-inflammatory, antimicrobial, antibacterial and antifungal food source with no side effects! Sounds like edible gold to me!

Nutrition Facts

Serv. Size 3 oz (85g)
Calories 50
Fat Cal. 35

Amount/serving	%DV*	Amount/serving	%DV*
Total Fat 4g	6%	**Total Carb.** 4g	1%
Sat. Fat 0.5g	3%	Fiber 1g	5%
Trans Fat 0g		Sugars 2g	
Cholest. 0mg	0%	**Protein** 1g	
Sodium 20mg	1%		

*Percent Daily Values (DV) are based on a 2,000 calorie diet.

Vitamin A 90% • Vitamin C 20% • Calcium 2% • Iron 4%

4
Minutes

8 Minutes

TANGY DIJON MUSTARD SALAD

SERVES 2

1) 3 TBSP Extra Virgin Olive Oil
2) 1 tsp Aged Balsamic Vinegar (my favorite is Villa Manodori)
3) Salt and Pepper, to taste
4) Dash of Curry Powder
5) ½ tsp Dijon Mustard
6) 2 TBSP Pomegranate Seeds
7) 1 Bag Mixed Greens (made up of baby spinach, chicory, and dill)

Place ingredients 1-5 in a bowl. Whisk for 20 seconds and allow it to rest for three minutes. You want to give the ingredients time to get to know each other. Add ingredients 6 and 7 and toss well.

To put stilettos on this dish – Olives could easily take this salad to another level; remember they tend to be salty so compensate for salt usage by using less salt in the first step. To remove pits from olives, use the heel of your hand and push down on the olive. The pit will easily slide out. Chop them up and add to the salad.

Nutrition Facts	Amount/serving	%DV*	Amount/serving	%DV*
Serv. Size 2 oz (57g)	**Total Fat** 5g	8%	**Total Carb.** 3g	1%
Calories 60	Sat. Fat 0.5g	4%	Fiber 2g	6%
Fat Cal. 45	*Trans* Fat 0g		Sugars 1g	
	Cholest. 0mg	0%	**Protein** 1g	
	Sodium 30mg	1%		
*Percent Daily Values (DV) are based on a 2,000 calorie diet.	Vitamin A 80% • Vitamin C 70% • Calcium 8% • Iron 4%			

SANDWICHES

AVOCADO AND GOAT CHEESE ON EZEKIEL

BABY SPINACH SMOKED TURKEY WRAP

CRISPY CIABATTA WITH PROSCIUTTO AND MOZZARELLA

CRUNCHY PESTO VEGGIE PANINI

GREEN LEAFY WRAP WITH SMOKED SALMON

HUMMUS WRAP WITH SAUTÉED VEGGIES

NOT-YOUR-AVERAGE HAM AND CHEESE

PA' VOLVER A COMER

PORTOBELLO SHIITAKE WRAP WITH SWEET ONIONS

TOASTED PANINI WITH AVOCADO AND CHEESE

SMOKED SALMON WITH CHEESE

4 Minutes

AVOCADO AND GOAT CHEESE ON EZEKIEL

SERVES 2

1) 2 Slices of Ezekiel Bread
2) 2 tsp Spreadable Goat Cheese
3) $^1/_2$ Avocado (thinly sliced)
4) 1 Small Tomato (thinly sliced)
5) Salt and Pepper, to taste
6) 2 TBSP Alfalfa Sprouts (any sprout will do)
7) 1 Slice Cheddar Cheese (try Organic Valley)

Spread goat cheese on both slices of bread. Place sliced avocado on top. Layer on the tomato, salt, pepper, sprouts, and slice of cheese. Place second slice of bread on top and press down.

To make it crispy ~ Drizzle quality extra virgin olive oil on the bread and toast it in a George Foreman grill or skillet. Serve with corn chips that are made from either sunflower oil or peanut oil. Garnish with parsley and don't forget to eat it! Parsley is great for digestion and can help with bad breath by eliminating acid in the stomach.

Nutrition Facts	Amount/serving	%DV*	Amount/serving	%DV*
Serv. Size 7 oz (198g)	Total Fat 17g	25%	Total Carb. 38g	13%
	Sat. Fat 3.5g	16%	Fiber 13g	53%
Calories 340	*Trans* Fat 0g		Sugars 0g	
Fat Cal. 150	Cholest. 5mg	1%	Protein 14g	
	Sodium 220mg	9%		
*Percent Daily Values (DV) are based on a 2,000 calorie diet.	Vitamin A 4% • Vitamin C 25% • Calcium 6% • Iron 10%			

BABY SPINACH SMOKED TURKEY WRAP

SERVES 1

1) 1 Whole Wheat or Gluten-Free Wrap
2) ½ Small Onion (thinly sliced)
3) Dash of Spike Seasoning
4) 2 Slices Smoked Turkey (shredded)
5) 5 Baby Spinach Leaves
6) 1 tsp Mayonnaise
7) 1 Small Cucumber or Pickle (thinly sliced)
8) 2 slices Cheddar Cheese (try Cotswold with chives)

Lay wrap out on a flat surface. Spread mayonnaise on wrap. In center of wrap, layer cucumbers, onions, turkey, spinach, and cheese and sprinkle with a dash of seasoning. Roll it up. Slice in half or on an angle for a nice presentation.

To make it succulent ~ Add a chopped bell pepper. You can replace the turkey with shredded tofu, the mayonnaise with honey mustard, and the cheddar with provolone. Have some fun! Go ahead and try to make up your own variation of the recipe!

Nutrition Facts

Serv. Size 6 oz (170g)

Calories 250

Fat Cal. 100

*Percent Daily Values (DV) are based on a 2,000 calorie diet.

Amount/serving	%DV*	Amount/serving	%DV*
Total Fat 11g	17%	Total Carb. 24g	8%
Sat. Fat 5g	26%	Fiber 5g	20%
Trans Fat 0g		Sugars 2g	
Cholest. 40mg	13%	Protein 17g	
Sodium 450mg	19%		

Vitamin A 4% • Vitamin C 15% • Calcium 20% • Iron 20%

9 Minutes

CRISPY CIABATTA WITH PROSCIUTTO AND MOZZARELLA

SERVES 2

1) 2 Slices of Ciabatta Bread
2) 1 tsp Mayonnaise
3) 2 Slices Prosciutto di Parma
4) 2 Slices Mozzarella Cheese
5) 1 Small Tomato (sliced)
6) 2 Green Lettuce Leaves
7) 3 Sandwich Pickle Slices
8) 1 tsp Extra Virgin Olive Oil

Spread mayonnaise on both slices of bread. Place ingredients 3-7 on top of one slice and add the second slice. Drizzle with olive oil and press in a George Foreman grill, or any grill that you have, for six minutes. If using a skillet instead of a grill, I would recommend using sunflower oil instead of extra virgin olive oil see page 13 for which oils are best to eat. In this case, use your spatula to press down and toast each side for one minute.

To make this divine ~ Replace the mozzarella with buffalo mozzarella. Many people have never heard of buffalo mozzarella (it may also be labeled "mozzarella di bufala"). It's made from buffalo's milk and it's divine! With a hard outer shell and a soft, creamy inside, it makes for a great complement to any sandwich.

Nutrition Facts	Amount/serving	%DV*	Amount/serving	%DV*
Serv. Size 8 oz (227g)	Total Fat 10g	16%	Total Carb. 44g	15%
	Sat. Fat 4.5g	23%	Fiber 2g	8%
Calories 340	Trans Fat 0g		Sugars 0g	
Fat Cal. 90	Cholest. 35mg	12%	Protein 17g	
	Sodium 350mg	14%		
*Percent Daily Values (DV) are based on a 2,000 calorie diet.	Vitamin A 10% • Vitamin C 20% • Calcium 20% • Iron 15%			

CRUNCHY PESTO VEGGIE PANINI

SERVES 2

1) 2 Slices Whole Wheat or Gluten-Free Bread
2) 1 TBSP Pesto
3) 4 Slices of Zucchini
4) 3 Eggplant Slices
5) 1 tsp Extra Virgin Olive Oil (infused if you can find it)
6) 5 Baby Arugula Leaves

Spread pesto on both slices of bread. Using a mandolin, thinly slice the zucchini (vertically) and eggplant. Layer evenly on one slice of bread and add arugula. Close panini and drizzle with extra virgin olive oil. Then place in George Foreman grill, or a skillet. If you are using a skillet, I would suggest using a tsp of butter instead of the extra virgin olive oil. Toast until golden brown then cut on an angle. To plate: set one half in center of plate and rest the other half slightly on an angle overlapping the other. Garnish with one of my side dishes or complete it with some killer quality chips.

To make it velvety ~ Slice your favorite cheese - whether it is manchego from (Spain), gruyere from (Switzerland) or any unpasteurized cheese, and add to your sandwich. Thin slices of cheese can be used to help the panini stay together and to prevent the oil from leaking out. Combine veggies in your food processor. Pulse for five seconds and spread mixture on top of the cheese. Then toast to your desired liking.

Nutrition Facts

Serv. Size 7 oz (198g)

Calories 350
Fat Cal. 110

Amount/serving	%DV*	Amount/serving	%DV*
Total Fat 12g	19%	**Total Carb.** 52g	17%
Sat. Fat 1g	6%	Fiber 6g	23%
Trans Fat 0g		Sugars 2g	
Cholest. 0mg	0%	**Protein** 11g	
Sodium 5mg	0%		

*Percent Daily Values (DV) are based on a 2,000 calorie diet.

Vitamin A 60% • Vitamin C 20% • Calcium 8% • Iron 30%

10
Minutes

3 Minutes

GREEN LEAFY WRAP WITH SMOKED SALMON

SERVES 1

1) 3 oz. Smoked Salmon
2) 1 Large Swiss Chard Leaf
3) 1 TBSP Spreadable Goat Cheese
4) Dash of Pepper
5) Dash of Curry Powder
6) 1 tsp Extra Virgin Olive Oil
7) 1 tsp Ginger (shredded on grater)
8) 5 Cherry Tomatoes (sliced in half)

Lay leaf on a flat surface. Arbitrarily spread goat cheese on it with the back of a spoon. Rest salmon on top. If you prefer, you may substitute shredded turkey or tofu in place of the smoked salmon. Add tomatoes and sprinkle with pepper, curry powder and ginger. Then, drizzle with extra virgin olive oil. Wrap it up and enjoy!

Eat this ~ Curry powder is typically made from three spices: turmeric (which gives it the yellow appearance) cumin and coriander. This combination is not always exact; many other spices are often added to this blend. Curry powder is an antioxidant and an anti-inflammatory.

Nutrition Facts	Amount/serving	%DV*	Amount/serving	%DV*
Serv. Size 6 oz (170g)	**Total Fat** 16g	**25%**	**Total Carb.** 3g	**1%**
Calories 270	Sat. Fat 4.5g	21%	Fiber 1g	4%
Fat Cal. 140	*Trans* Fat 0g		Sugars 1g	
	Cholest. 75mg	**25%**	**Protein** 28g	
	Sodium 230mg	**9%**		
*Percent Daily Values (DV) are based on a 2,000 calorie diet.	Vitamin A 70% • Vitamin C 25% • Calcium 6% • Iron 15%			

HUMMUS WRAP WITH SAUTÉED VEGGIES

SERVES ABOUT 1 ½

1) 1 Whole Wheat or Gluten-Free Wrap
2) 1 TBSP Hummus
3) ½ Spanish Onion
4) ½ Red Pepper (diced)
5) 5 Slices Summer Squash
6) Handful of Baby Spinach
7) 1 TBSP Hemp Oil
8) 1 tsp Almond Oil (optional)

This wrap is really easy to make and fun to eat during my favorite time of the year: NFL season. There are two meanings to NFL. One is National Football League, and for those who don't like football in my house, the acronym stands for Not For Long. In any case, you will enjoy this sandwich.

On your mandolin, thinly slice onion and squash. Heat your skillet and sauté ingredients 3-6 for three minutes. Bring your wrap to room temperature or heat it in your skillet. Spread the hummus on the wrap and distribute vegetables from the skillet on top. To finish, drizzle with hemp oil and almond oil. Roll it up! If you'd like, add mint, cilantro or marjoram and a hint of lime or lemon.

Eat this ~ Hummus is a Middle Eastern food composed of chickpeas, or garbanzo beans, and tahini. Tahini is a paste similar in texture to peanut butter, but made from sesame seeds. Chickpeas are a good source of protein, potassium and fiber. Sesame seeds also contain protein, vitamin E and powerful antioxidants. Because both chickpeas and sesame seeds are wonderfully healthy, hummus is a nutritionist's delight!

Nutrition Facts

Serv. Size 5 oz (142g)

Calories 240
Fat Cal. 120

*Percent Daily Values (DV) are based on a 2,000 calorie diet.

Amount/serving	%DV*	Amount/serving	%DV*
Total Fat 14g	21%	Total Carb. 25g	8%
Sat. Fat 2g	9%	Fiber 5g	18%
Trans Fat 0g		Sugars 2g	
Cholest. 0mg	0%	Protein 7g	
Sodium 160mg	7%		
Vitamin A 2% • Vitamin C 50% • Calcium 4% • Iron 15%			

8 Minutes

10 Minutes

NOT-YOUR-AVERAGE HAM AND CHEESE

SERVES ABOUT 1 ½

1) 2 Slices Bread (gluten-free or unbleached)
2) 2 Slices Uncured Ham (shredded)
3) 2 Slices Gruyere Cheese
4) 6 Baby Spinach Leaves
5) 1 tsp Extra Virgin Olive Oil

Drizzle bread with the extra virgin olive oil. Then, layer ingredients 2-4 on one slice of bread. Place the other slice on top and press down. Place sandwich in your skillet, press down with your spatula and toast each side. Once the cheese has melted, your masterpiece is done and ready for your teeth to sink into it. Trim off the ends and cut into quarters. Always look at your dish and ask yourself, "what might make this better?". At times, it might just be as simple as toasting it.

Eat This ~ The ham makes up 346mg of the sodium and the gruyere contributes to 14mg of the fat content. For healthy alternatives, replace the ham with shredded smoked turkey and replace the cheese with skim, or vegan cheese.

Nutrition Facts	Amount/serving	%DV*	Amount/serving	%DV*
Serv. Size 6 oz (170g)	**Total Fat** 17g	**25%**	**Total Carb.** 55g	**18%**
Calories 470	Sat. Fat 8g	**38%**	Fiber 2g	**10%**
Fat Cal. 150	*Trans* Fat 0g		Sugars 0g	
	Cholest. 50mg	**17%**	**Protein** 25g	
	Sodium 440mg	**19%**		
*Percent Daily Values (DV) are based on a 2,000 calorie diet.	Vitamin A 70% • Vitamin C 15% • Calcium 40% • Iron 25%			

SERVES ABOUT 1 ½

1) 1 TBSP Sunflower Oil
2) ¼ Onion (thinly sliced)
3) ¼ Red Pepper (sliced)
4) 1 Slice Cheese (use your favorite)
5) 1 Slice Turkey Breast (diced)
6) 1 TBSP Salsa
7) 1 Wrap

Heat sunflower oil in a hot skillet. Add ingredients 2 and 3 and cook for five minutes. Add salsa and continue to cook for one minute. During that time, place cheese and turkey on wrap. Then, lay the ingredients from the skillet on top and roll it up.

To make it wholesome ~ Whole grain bread is indeed better for digestion than white bread. Also, try replacing salsa with pesto and substitue the turkey for one of Ian's products options (meat-free, gluten-free, soy-free). Most of these meat alternatives are frozen, so cooking time will vary. Season wrap with your favorite infused oil or condiment. You will cut the sodium in half if you load up on vegetables and decrease the amount of meat.

Nutrition Facts	Amount/serving	%DV*	Amount/serving	%DV*
Serv. Size 7 oz (198g)	**Total Fat** 28g	**43%**	**Total Carb.** 49g	**16%**
Calories 520	**Sat.** Fat 8g	**42%**	Fiber 7g	**29%**
Fat Cal. 250	*Trans* Fat 0g		Sugars 3g	
	Cholest. 30mg	**11%**	**Protein** 26g	
	Sodium 240mg	**10%**		
*Percent Daily Values (DV) are based on a 2,000 calorie diet.	Vitamin A 6% • Vitamin C 15% • Calcium 50% • Iron 30%			

10 Minutes

9 Minutes

PORTOBELLO SHIITAKE WRAP WITH SWEET ONIONS

SERVES ABOUT 1 ½

1) 1 TBSP Sunflower Oil
2) 1 Shallot
3) 1 Portobello Mushroom
4) ¼ Red Pepper
5) 8 Shiitake Mushrooms
6) 1 Clove of Garlic
7) Dash of Spike Seasoning
8) 1 Whole Wheat or Gluten-Free Wrap
9) ½ tsp Extra Virgin Olive Oil

On medium to high heat, warm sunflower oil in skillet. In your food processor, combine ingredients 2–6 and pulse for four seconds. Remove and place in skillet. Add seasoning and cook for five to seven minutes. Lay out wrap and drizzle with extra virgin olive oil. Spread vegetable mixture on the wrap, and roll it up.

To make this fresh ~ Add as much cilantro, parsley or mint as you can take! It will complement the mushrooms and shallot. You could also spread a TBSP of hummus on the wrap before adding the vegetables.

Nutrition Facts	Amount/serving	%DV*	Amount/serving	%DV*
Serv. Size 6 oz (170g)	**Total Fat** 11g	**17%**	**Total Carb.** 44g	**15%**
Calories 280	Sat. Fat 1g	6%	Fiber 7g	27%
Fat Cal. 90	Trans Fat 0g		Sugars 6g	
	Cholest. 0mg	0%	**Protein** 9g	
	Sodium 105mg	4%		
*Percent Daily Values (DV) are based on a 2,000 calorie diet.	Vitamin A 2% • Vitamin C 50% • Calcium 4% • Iron 15%			

SERVES 2

1) 2 Slices Ezekiel Bread
2) ½ Avocado
3) 2 Slices of American Cheese or Mozzarella
4) 1 tsp Mayonnaise
5) 5 Sprigs of Cilantro
6) Salt and Pepper, to taste
7) 1 tsp Sunflower Oil

Slice avocado in ¼-inch pieces. Spread mayonnaise evenly on both slices of bread and place one slice of cheese on bread along with your cut avocado. Then add salt, pepper, cilantro and the second slice of cheese. Close sandwich by placing the second slice of bread on top. Put sunflower oil and panini in skillet and press down on it with spatula. On high heat, toast each side for one minute. Remove from skillet and cut in half. To plate: set one half in center of plate and rest the other half slightly on an angle overlapping it. If you have a George Foreman grill, or any grill for that matter, feel free to use it instead of the skillet. I usually place a 5 lb weight on top of the grill so the sandwich can turn into a tasty panini.Give Ezekiel bread a try; it's sprouty, full of whole grains, and wonderful in a panini.

To give it VIP status ~ Spread pesto on the inside of each slice before toasting it. This will increase the amount of fat - so keep it healthy by reducing the amount of cheese. I would not add any additional salt to the sandwich.

Nutrition Facts

Serv. Size 7 oz (198g)

Calories 470

Fat Cal. 220

Amount/serving	%DV*	Amount/serving	%DV*
Total Fat 25g	38%	Total Carb. 40g	13%
Sat. Fat 7g	36%	Fiber 13g	53%
Trans Fat 0g		Sugars 1g	
Cholest. 20mg	7%	Protein 24g	
Sodium 230mg	9%		

*Percent Daily Values (DV) are based on a 2,000 calorie diet.

Vitamin A 25% • Vitamin C 15% • Calcium 30% • Iron 10%

8 Minutes

SMOKED SALMON WITH CHEESE

SERVES ABOUT 1 ½

1) 1 Whole Wheat or Gluten-Free Wrap
2) 1 tsp Mayonnaise
3) 1 oz. Shredded Manchego Cheese
4) 6 Baby Spinach Leaves
5) Dash of Spike Seasoning
6) 4 oz. Smoked Salmon
7) 1 tsp Extra Virgin Olive Oil

In a heated skillet, warm both sides of wrap for about thirty seconds each. Remove from skillet and spread mayonnaise on top. Then layer with ingredients 3-6. Drizzle with extra virgin olive oil. To finish, roll it up. Serve with my Jazzed Up Chips (found on page 157). Rock'n Roll!

To make it stand out ~ Ginger root (rich in vitamin A) and sardines make a great combination. On your grater, shred ⅛ inch of ginger root and mix that in with the mayonnaise. You can always replace the fish with sardines, anchovies or shredded rotisserie chicken.

Eat this ~ Manchego cheese is a raw sheep's milk cheese made in the La Mancha region of Spain. It's aged 3 months (sometimes longer), and is a semi-firm cheese with a rich golden color.

Nutrition Facts	Amount/serving	%DV*	Amount/serving	%DV*
Serv. Size 6 oz (170g)	Total Fat 20g	31%	Total Carb. 24g	8%
	Sat. Fat 3.5g	17%	Fiber 4g	16%
Calories 360	Trans Fat 0g		Sugars 0g	
Fat Cal. 180	Cholest. 50mg	16%	Protein 24g	
	Sodium 220mg	9%		
*Percent Daily Values (DV) are based on a 2,000 calorie diet.	Vitamin A 80% • Vitamin C 25% • Calcium 8% • Iron 20%			

PASTA

BUTTERNUT RAVIOLI WITH PARMIGIANO

BUTTERNUT SAGE SAUCE

CHEESE RAVIOLI WITH CREAMY DELICATA SHAVINGS

CRESTE DI GALLO WITH PESTO

ORGANIC RAVIOLI WITH BROCCOLI FLORETS

TURKEY SAUSAGE WITH RAVIOLI

WICKED FAST TOMATO SAUCE

10 Minutes

BUTTERNUT RAVIOLI WITH PARMIGIANO

SERVES ABOUT 1 ½

1) 2 TBSP Sunflower Oil
2) 1 Small Spanish Onion (thinly sliced on mandolin)
3) 1 Clove of Garlic (diced)
4) ¼ C. Vegetable Broth
5) Shake of Curry Powder
6) 1 Package Butternut Squash Ravioli (fresh)
7) 1 TBSP Parmigiano Cheese
8) Handful of Baby Spinach
9) 1 tsp Extra Virgin Olive Oil
10) ¼ Lemon (juice and zest)

In a hot skillet, heat sunflower oil and combine ingredients 2–5. Stir and cook for three minutes. Combine fresh ravioli and cook for an additional five minutes. If your skillet starts to dry up, just add liquid (an additional ¼ C. of vegetable broth in small amounts should do the trick). Finally, combine cheese and spinach in the skillet. To plate: garnish with extra virgin olive oil and the zest and juice of ¼ lemon.

You should be able to find fresh ravioli in most grocery stores. If not, you can use frozen and follow the same instructions. Be sure to just thaw them out.

To make it meaty ~ Remove the casing from two turkey, beef or pork sausage links and sauté with the onion and garlic. If you like kale, I'd add 1 C. of chopped kale and allow it to wilt during the cooking process. Enjoy it with a bottle of champagne. My favorite is Laurent-Perrier, But remember - everything in moderation my friends.

Nutrition Facts	Amount/serving	%DV*	Amount/serving	%DV*
Serv. Size 6 oz (170g)	**Total Fat** 15g	23%	**Total Carb.** 7g	2%
Calories 170	**Sat. Fat** 1.5g	8%	Fiber 2g	8%
Fat Cal. 130	*Trans* Fat 0g		Sugars 2g	
	Cholest. 0mg	0%	**Protein** 4g	
	Sodium 230mg	10%		
*Percent Daily Values (DV) are based on a 2,000 calorie diet.	Vitamin A 140% • Vitamin C 40% • Calcium 10% • Iron 15%			

BUTTERNUT SAGE SAUCE

SERVES 1

1) ³/₄ C. Butternut Squash (pre-cut)
2) 1 Stalk Burdock Root
3) 1 Clove of Garlic
4) 1 tsp Sunflower Oil
5) 1 C. Vegetable or Chicken Broth
6) ½ Spanish Onion (Diced)
7) Sea Salt and Fresh Pepper, to taste
8) ¼ C. Sliced Almonds
9) Pinch of Curry Powder or Cayenne Pepper
10) 6 Sage Leaves (coarsely chopped)

This is an awesome, autumn sauce for fresh, frozen, whole wheat or gluten-free ricotta ravioli. It can also be used in a cold pasta salad.

Combine ingredients 1–3 in a food processor and pulse for four to eight seconds, depending on your texture preference. In a hot skillet, heat sunflower oil, add ingredients 5–7 and cook for two minutes. Remove squash mixture from food processor and incorporate in hot skillet. Sauté and stir for six minutes. Add ingredients 8–10 and cook for two more minutes.

To wow your guests ~ Add 4 to 5 sun-dried tomatoes. They will add color, richness and a full flavor to the dish. If you'd like to make it creamy, add ¼ C. of heavy cream.

Nutrition Facts	Amount/serving	%DV*	Amount/serving	%DV*
Serv. Size 6 oz (170g)	Total Fat 10g	15%	Total Carb. 21g	7%
Calories 180	Sat. Fat 1g	4%	Fiber 5g	19%
Fat Cal. 90	Trans Fat 0g		Sugars 4g	
	Cholest. 0mg	0%	Protein 5g	
	Sodium 5mg	0%		
*Percent Daily Values (DV) are based on a 2,000 calorie diet.	Vitamin A 240% • Vitamin C 45% • Calcium 10% • Iron 10%			

10 Minutes

10 Minutes

CHEESE RAVIOLI WITH CREAMY DELICATA SHAVINGS

SERVES ABOUT 1

1) 2 TBSP of Sunflower Oil
2) 1 Shallot (diced)
3) 6 Cherry Tomatoes (sliced in half)
4) 1 tsp Rosemary
5) 8 Cheese Ravioli (fresh or frozen)
6) Dash of Spike Seasoning
7) ½ C. Vegetable Broth
8) 1 TBSP Crème Fraîche or Sour Cream
9) 1 Delicata Squash
10) 1 tsp Extra Virgin Olive Oil

In skillet, heat sunflower oil and combine ingredients 2-6. In the meantime, peel skin from squash using a mandolin, then slice vertically. You will want about 5 thin slices. Once sliced, dice into ¼ inch pieces. Add ingredients 7-9, and cook for an additional four minutes. To plate: create a bed with the liquid mixture, rest ravioli on the bed. Garnish with extra virgin olive oil.

To make it smile ~ Add a few crushed cashews or your favorite nut – it's a crunchy way to finish the dish. However, don't go nuts - whatever you can fit in your hand is the maximum amount you should eat.

Nutrition Facts	Amount/serving	%DV*	Amount/serving	%DV*
Serv. Size 7 oz (198g)	Total Fat 15g	23%	Total Carb. 8g	3%
Calories 170	Sat. Fat 1.5g	8%	Fiber 2g	6%
Fat Cal. 130	Trans Fat 0g		Sugars 3g	
	Cholest. 0mg	0%	Protein 2g	
	Sodium 160mg	7%		
*Percent Daily Values (DV) are based on a 2,000 calorie diet.	Vitamin A 15% • Vitamin C 35% • Calcium 2% • Iron 4%			

CRESTE DI GALLO WITH PESTO

SERVES ABOUT 3

1) ¾ C. Fresh Pasta (best if Creste di Gallo Pasta)
2) 1 C. Peas (frozen)
3) 1 TBSP Pesto
4) 2 ½ C. Water
5) 1 Egg
6) ¼ Lemon (juice)
7) 1 tsp Extra Virgin Olive Oil

Creste di Gallo looks like a rooster's comb or octopus tentacles, and comes from an area that I call the "Achilles tendon of Italy" (a.k.a. Apulia, or "the heel"). It's made from the finest durum flour, which allows sauces to cling to every delicious bite because of its comb-like texture.

Boil water in a pot on high heat. This should take about six minutes. Once boiling, add pasta and cook for two minutes. Add peas to water and cook for an additional minute. Turn off heat, strain pasta and peas and place them back into the same pot, returning them to the hot burner. Crack egg into pot and stir in pesto. The egg will cook in thirty seconds. To finish, squeeze lemon juice and drizzle extra virgin olive oil over the top.

To make it dance ~ Dice 1 or 2 plum tomatoes and add to the hot pot with the egg. To garnish, add a few red peppercorns for a nice finish.

Eat this ~ Finding pesto without pine nuts decreases the amount of fat from 26 grams to 13 grams. That's right... pine nuts are high in fat, just some food for thought.

Nutrition Facts	Amount/serving	%DV*	Amount/serving	%DV*
Serv. Size 6 oz (170g)	Total Fat 15g	23%	Total Carb. 18g	6%
	Sat. Fat 2.5g	12%	Fiber 3g	14%
Calories 250	Trans Fat 0g		Sugars 1g	
Fat Cal. 130	Cholest. 15mg	5%	Protein 10g	
	Sodium 140mg	6%		
*Percent Daily Values (DV) are based on a 2,000 calorie diet.	Vitamin A 70% • Vitamin C 40% • Calcium 15% • Iron 20%			

9 Minutes

10 Minutes

ORGANIC RAVIOLI WITH BROCCOLI FLORETS

SERVES ABOUT 1 ½

1) 2 TBSP Sunflower Oil
2) 8 Organic Ravioli (fresh or frozen)
3) ½ Spanish Onion (sliced on mandolin)
4) ¾ C. Vegetable Broth
5) 1 C. Broccoli Florets (use only the florets, the tiny green buds at the end of the stalks)
6) 2 Cloves of Garlic (minced)
7) 1 tsp Chipotle Sauce
8) Dash of Spike Seasoning
9) 5 Chives (finely chopped)
10) 1 tsp Parmesan Shavings

Heat sunflower oil for one minute on high heat. Sauté ingredients 2–6 and cook for four minutes. Ravioli can be filled with cheese, butternut squash, or meat - it's your choice. Combine ingredients 7 and 8 and cook for three additional minutes. If you need more liquid, feel free to use leftover brine, water, wine, or more broth. Finally, add chives for garnish and top it off with parmesan cheese shavings.

To make it snazzy ~ I love to garnish by drizzling a drop of Villa Mandori Balsamic Vinegar over it. It's wicked expensive, but worth every penny. All you need is a little – a few drops go a long way. Be sure to get every last drop by turning the bottle upside down overnight and using the cap full of vinegar in your next creation! For a crunch, you can add 5 to 8 pine nuts as garnish.

Nutrition Facts

Serv. Size 6 oz (170g)

Calories 140

Fat Cal. 100

Amount/serving	%DV*	Amount/serving	%DV*
Total Fat 11g	17%	Total Carb. 11g	4%
Sat. Fat 1g	6%	Fiber 3g	11%
Trans Fat 0g		Sugars 3g	
Cholest. 0mg	0%	Protein 3g	
Sodium 130mg	5%		

*Percent Daily Values (DV) are based on a 2,000 calorie diet.

Vitamin A 10% • Vitamin C 130% • Calcium 6% • Iron 4%

TURKEY SAUSAGE WITH RAVIOLI

SERVES ABOUT 1 ½

1) 2 TBSP Sunflower Oil
2) 1 Spanish Onion (diced)
3) 1 Clove of Garlic (diced)
4) ⅔ C. Vegetable Broth
5) Dash of Curry Powder
6) 2–3 oz. Turkey Sausage (de-cased and broken up)
7) 5 Fresh Vegetable Ravioli
8) 1 TBSP Grated Parmigiano-Reggiano
9) Handful of Baby Spinach
10) 1 tsp Extra Virgin Olive Oil

In a hot skillet, heat sunflower oil and combine ingredients 2–5. Stir while cooking for three minutes or until onion is softened. Add ingredients 6 and 7 to the skillet. Cook for five minutes or until the sausage is done. It always helps to have extra broth or stock on hand in case the skillet becomes dry. Finally, combine ingredients 8 and 9 in the skillet and cook for one more minute. Plate and garnish by drizzling the extra virgin olive oil over the top.

Eat this ~ Choosing meatless products can lower cholesterol, lessen the risk of heart disease and help aid in proper digestion. Check out products like Boca Foods, Alexia Foods, Health is Wealth or Ian's foods. Keep reading your labels and if you don't understand anything, ask questions or Google it. It's your health and it should not be compromised.

Nutrition Facts

Serv. Size 6 oz (170g)
Calories 230
Fat Cal. 150

Amount/serving	%DV*	Amount/serving	%DV*
Total Fat 16g	25%	Total Carb. 15g	5%
Sat. Fat 2.5g	13%	Fiber 1g	5%
Trans Fat 0g		Sugars 1g	
Cholest. 15mg	5%	Protein 6g	
Sodium 400mg	17%		

*Percent Daily Values (DV) are based on a 2,000 calorie diet.

Vitamin A 70%	•	Vitamin C 20%	•	Calcium 8%	•	Iron 10%

10 Minutes

8 Minutes

WICKED FAST TOMATO SAUCE

SERVES ABOUT 2

1) 1 Clove of Garlic
2) 5 Kalamata Olives (pitted)
3) Sea Salt and Fresh Pepper, to taste
4) 1 Shallot
5) 1 TBSP Flat Leaf Parsley
6) 3 Medium Sized Tomatoes
7) 2 TBSP Sunflower Oil

Combine ingredients 1–6 in your food processor and pulse for four seconds. Take out and add to pre-heated skillet with sunflower oil. Cook and stir for eight minutes. If you'd like to remove the excess water from the sauce, use your sieve to drain it. Another option is to simmer it for a longer time at a lower temperature and it will slowly evaporate.

To make this dish jump ~ Gnocchi, made from potato, is a great complement to this dish and is really easy. Four minutes after the sauce begins cooking, add this Italian dumpling. Feel free to combine peas, corn or capers. You could also roll in 1 tsp of miso after the cooking process and totally change the dish again!

Nutrition Facts	Amount/serving	%DV*	Amount/serving	%DV*
Serv. Size 6 oz (170g)	Total Fat 13g	20%	Total Carb. 21g	7%
	Sat. Fat 1.5g	7%	Fiber 1g	4%
Calories 210	Trans Fat 0g		Sugars 0g	
Fat Cal. 110	Cholest. 0mg	0%	Protein 4g	
	Sodium 250mg	10%		
*Percent Daily Values (DV) are based on a 2,000 calorie diet.	Vitamin A 4% • Vitamin C 25% • Calcium 2% • Iron 6%			

FISH

CITRUS SALMON WITH GREENS

CITRUS SIMMERED SCALLOPS WITH BABY GREENS

SAVORY SUMMER SOLE WITH A RICOTTA FILLING

SEARED TUNA WITH CASHEW CRUSTED TOPPING

SEARED TUNA WITH WALNUT PUREE

10 Minutes

LEMON PEPPER SALMON WITH GREENS

SERVES 3

1) 1 TBSP Sunflower Oil
2) 1 tsp Thyme
3) ½ Spanish Onion (thinly sliced on mandolin)
4) Salt and Pepper, to taste
5) 4 oz. Wild Salmon
6) 1 Kale Leaf (chopped)
7) 1 Swiss Chard Leaf (chopped)
8) ¼ Meyer Lemon (juice)
9) 3 Chives (chopped)
10) ½ C. Vegetable Broth

Season salmon on both sides with thyme, salt and pepper. In a hot skillet, heat sunflower oil. Add onions and cook for two minutes. Rest the salmon on the onions, cover and cook on low heat for three minutes. With salmon, undercooking is always better than overcooking. When skillet becomes dry, add broth. Add ingredients 6–8 and continue to cook until greens wilt. To plate: rest bed of greens in the center of a plate, then place fish on top. Garnish with chives.

To make it charming ~ Add 1 tsp of honey to the cooking process. Juniper berries are also a nice garnish to this dish. These berries have a pungent and piney flavor that lends itself well to herbs.

Nutrition Facts	Amount/serving	%DV*	Amount/serving	%DV*
Serv. Size 5 oz (142g)	Total Fat 10g	16%	Total Carb. 7g	2%
	Sat. Fat 1g	4%	Fiber 1g	6%
Calories 150	Trans Fat 0g		Sugars 1g	
Fat Cal. 90	Cholest. 20mg	6%	Protein 9g	
	Sodium 125mg	5%		
*Percent Daily Values (DV) are based on a 2,000 calorie diet.	Vitamin A 140% • Vitamin C 90% • Calcium 8% • Iron 10%			

10 Minutes

SAVORY SUMMER SOLE WITH A RICOTTA FILLING

SERVES 2

Ricotta Filling:
1) ½ Cup Ricotta Cheese
2) 1 tsp Pine Nuts
3) 4 Sprigs of Tarragon (chopped)
4) 1 Clove of Garlic (diced)
5) 2 tsp Italian Bread Crumbs

Sole:
1) ¼ Spanish Onion (thinly sliced)
2) ¼ Yellow Tomato (chopped)
3) 1 tsp Sunflower Oil
4) Salt and Pepper, to taste
5) ¼ C. Edamame Beans
6) ½ C. Vegetable Broth
7) 8 oz. Sole

For the Filling:

In a bowl, mix all 5 ingredients together and reserve.

For the Sole:

Combine the first 5 ingredients in a skillet on high heat. Wait one minute and lower the heat just a little, then slowly add the vegetable broth a little at a time. Let sit for about three minutes to give the ingredients a chance to dance, then stir. Cut sole in half and place both pieces on top of vegetables and cook for another minute or two.

To warm the filling just a little, scoop out of bowl and place on the side of the skillet. Remove from heat after one minute. To finish, place vegetables on plate, then center half of the sole on that bed. Place warm filling on top of the filet and then place the other half of the sole on top. Garnish with sprouts, scallions or lemon zest.

Nutrition Facts	Amount/serving	%DV*	Amount/serving	%DV*
Serv. Size 7 oz (198g)	**Total Fat** 7g	**11%**	**Total Carb.** 23g	**8%**
Calories 210	Sat. Fat 1.5g	**7%**	Fiber 7g	**29%**
Fat Cal. 60	*Trans* Fat 0g		Sugars 2g	
	Cholest. 30mg	**9%**	**Protein** 18g	
	Sodium 230mg	**10%**		
*Percent Daily Values (DV) are based on a 2,000 calorie diet.	Vitamin A 4% • Vitamin C 25% • Calcium 20% • Iron 40%			

SEARED TUNA WITH CASHEW CRUSTED TOPPING

SERVES 2

1) ½ C. Cashews
2) 1 Clove of Garlic
3) 3 Mint Leaves
4) ¼ Lemon (juice and zest)
5) 2 TBSP Extra Virgin Olive Oil
6) Salt and Pepper, to taste
7) 8 oz. Tuna Steak
8) 1 tsp Butter or Sunflower Oil

Crust Topping:

Combine ingredients 1–5 in a food processor. Pulse four times, for five seconds each time. Remove and set aside.

For the Fish:

In a hot skillet, heat sunflower oil or butter. Season both sides of the tuna with salt and pepper and place in skillet. Cook each side for two to three minutes. If you like it rare, cook it for less time. Once tuna is cooked to desired texture (it is ok if the center is still pink), remove from skillet and pat the cashew topping onto the fish. If you have any set aside, garnish with extra virgin olive oil, lemon zest or herbs.

To make it colorful ~ Don't wash the skillet just yet. Using your mandolin, shred 1/3 C. of raw radicchio. Place shredded radicchio in skillet and allow it to start absorbing the tuna flavors. If the skillet is too dry, add ¼ C. water, lemon juice or 1 tsp butter. Use radicchio as a bed for your crusted tuna. Radicchio is such an underestimated vegetable. It's low in sodium and has 15 percent of your daily protein!

Nutrition Facts	Amount/serving	%DV*	Amount/serving	%DV*
Serv. Size 4 oz (113g)	**Total Fat** 22g	**33%**	**Total Carb.** 2g	**1%**
Calories 260	Sat. Fat 2.5g	**12%**	Fiber 1g	**4%**
Fat Cal. 190	*Trans* Fat 0g		Sugars 0g	
	Cholest. 25mg	**9%**	**Protein** 16g	
	Sodium 90mg	**4%**		
*Percent Daily Values (DV) are based on a 2,000 calorie diet.	Vitamin A 0% • Vitamin C 2% • Calcium 2% • Iron 6%			

9 Minutes

10Minutes

SEARED TUNA WITH WALNUT PUREE

SERVES 2

1) ¼ C. Walnuts
2) 3 Sprigs of Tarragon
3) ¼ Lemon
4) 1 Clove of Garlic
5) 2 TBSP Extra Virgin Olive Oil
6) 1 TBSP Sunflower Oil
7) 8 oz. Tuna Steak
8) ½ tsp Spike Seasoning
9) Dash of Curry Powder
10) ⅓ C. Vegetable Broth

Combine ingredients 1-5 in food processor and pulse for six seconds. If it's not pasty in texture, add a few more drops of extra virgin olive oil.

In a hot skillet, heat sunflower oil. Season both sides of the tuna with ingredients 8 and 9 and place in skillet. After 10 seconds, use your rubber spatula to move the fish around to prevent it from searing to the skillet. Add half of the broth and cook for two minutes. Add the remaining broth if it becomes dry. Turn tuna over and place the walnut puree on top. Let sit for two minutes. Alternatives to broth include any liquid such as white wine, champagne or butter.

To make it gooda ~ Melt gouda on top of the tuna, drizzle olive oil over it and have your way with it! Gouda (from South Holland) is aged for 5 years, so the texture is semi-hard, yet it is still considerably creamier than other common cheeses. For a nice presentation, place 10 leaves of baby spinach on a plate, add a dash of balsamic vinegar and rest tuna on top.

Nutrition Facts	Amount/serving	%DV*	Amount/serving	%DV*
Serv. Size 4 oz (113g)	**Total Fat** 28g	**42%**	**Total Carb.** 4g	**1%**
Calories 320	Sat. Fat 3g	**15%**	Fiber 2g	**7%**
Fat Cal. 240	*Trans* Fat 0g		Sugars 1g	
	Cholest. 25mg	**8%**	**Protein** 16g	
	Sodium 80mg	**3%**		
*Percent Daily Values (DV) are based on a 2,000 calorie diet.	Vitamin A 0% • Vitamin C 2% • Calcium 4% • Iron 6%			

MEAT

BONELESS PORK LOIN WITH POMEGRANATE SAUCE

CHICKEN WITH GARLIC AND SWISS CHARD

EARTHY VEAL CUTLET

FETA SPINACH CHICKEN SAUSAGE WITH VEGGIES

SAUTÉED FILET MIGNON WITH PEPPERY PARSNIPS

TURKEY SAUSAGE WITH COLLARD GREENS

9 Minutes

BONELESS PORK LOIN WITH POMEGRANATE SAUCE

SERVES ABOUT 1

For the Pomegranate Sauce:
1) 2 TBSP Sunflower Oil
2) 1 Shallot (minced)
3) 1 TBSP Honey
4) 1 Clove of Garlic (minced)
5) 1 tsp of Rosemary (minced)
6) 1/3 C. Pomegranate Juice
7) 2 tsp Butter
8) 2 tsp Arrowroot or Flour

For the Pork:
9) Salt and Pepper, to taste
10) 6 oz. Boneless Pork Loin (1/2-inch thick)

You can substitute the pork for lean turkey or chicken cutlets. In a medium to hot skillet, combine ingredients 1–4 and sauté for two minutes. Add ingredients 5 and 6 and cook for one additional minute. Slowly stir in 1 tsp of butter and incorporate completely before adding the next tsp. Using a whisk, incorporate arrowroot or flour. Stir until sauce thickens. Next, season the pork loin with salt and pepper and place in sauce. After two minutes, turn over and cook for an additional minute. To plate: slice pork on an angle (you'll get about 6 to 8 slices out of it). This goes best with a bed of greens or mashed potatoes. For a killer presentation, fan out the meat and drizzle with extra virgin olive oil. Add a few pine nuts for a crunchy finish.

Eat this ~ Arrowroot looks and feels like flour, but it is not flour. It is a perennial herb that is easier to digest than white flour. Arrowroot is also gluten-free.

Nutrition Facts	Amount/serving	%DV*	Amount/serving	%DV*
Serv. Size 6 oz (170g)	Total Fat 29g	45%	Total Carb. 21g	7%
Calories 440	Sat. Fat 8g	40%	Fiber 0g	0%
Fat Cal. 260	*Trans* Fat 0g		Sugars 15g	
	Cholest. 80mg	27%	Protein 24g	
	Sodium 70mg	3%		
*Percent Daily Values (DV) are based on a 2,000 calorie diet.	Vitamin A 4% • Vitamin C 8% • Calcium 4% • Iron 6%			

SERVES ABOUT 1 ½

1) 3 TBSP Sunflower Oil
2) 2 Cloves of Chopped Garlic
3) 3 Vidalia Onions (sliced)
4) 1 TBSP Butter
5) Dash of Curry Powder
6) 1 TBSP Capers
7) 6 oz. Chicken Breast (chopped into small pieces)
8) Spike Seasoning, to taste
9) 2 Leaves Swiss Chard (finely chopped)
10) 1 tsp Extra Virgin Olive Oil

In a skillet, heat sunflower oil. Sauté ingredients 2-5 and cook for three minutes. Add ingredients 6-8 and cook for an additional three minutes. Lastly, rest the chard on top of the chicken and allow it to wilt - this should take about two minutes or less. Drizzle with extra virgin olive oil and serve.

To make it special ~ Toast a roll and fold this delicious mixture inside. I love this with a little chipotle sauce. To make this dish even easier, you can buy chicken that is already cooked and marinated. Try this with fish, turkey or ground beef. For folks who prefer tofu or meatless products, try Tofurky or Nate's products.

Nutrition Facts Serv. Size 6 oz (170g) **Calories** 260 Fat Cal. 150	Amount/serving	%DV*	Amount/serving	%DV*
	Total Fat 18g	**27**%	**Total Carb.** 6g	**2**%
	Sat. Fat 6g	**30**%	Fiber 1g	**5**%
	Trans Fat 0g		Sugars 2g	
	Cholest. 85mg	**29**%	**Protein** 19g	
	Sodium 130mg	**6**%		
*Percent Daily Values (DV) are based on a 2,000 calorie diet.	Vitamin A 35% • Vitamin C 30% • Calcium 4% • Iron 30%			

9 Minutes

6 Minutes

EARTHY VEAL CUTLET

SERVES ABOUT 1 ½

1) 2 TBSP Sunflower Oil
2) ½ lb Veal Cutlet (pounded thinly)
3) ¼ tsp Sage (chopped)
4) ¼ tsp Honey
5) 1 Shallot (diced)
6) ¼ tsp Balsamic Vinegar or Apple Cider Vinegar
7) ¼ Lemon (juice)
8) Salt and Pepper, to taste
9) Handful of Baby Spinach
10) 1 TBSP Extra Virgin Olive Oil

In a hot skillet, heat sunflower oil and add veal cutlet. Combine ingredients 3-8 in the skillet. Cook for three minutes. Turn over cutlet and cook for an additional minute.

In a bowl, combine ingredients 9 and 10 and toss well. Add a pinch of salt and pepper, if you'd like. To finish, plate greens in the center of a dish and rest ingredients from skillet on top. Drizzle juice from the skillet throughout.

To make it dance ~ Add 5 capers to it. A pinch of cayenne pepper will also give it a zing. You'll love it! Open a bottle of chardonnay. With its appley, buttery and nutty flavors as well as nuances of melons and pineapples, this will complement the dish exquisitely.

Nutrition Facts	Amount/serving	%DV*	Amount/serving	%DV*
Serv. Size 7 oz (198g)	Total Fat 14g	22%	Total Carb. 4g	1%
Calories 230	Sat. Fat 2g	11%	Fiber 2g	9%
Fat Cal. 120	Trans Fat 0g		Sugars 1g	
	Cholest. 70mg	23%	Protein 22g	
	Sodium 140mg	6%		
*Percent Daily Values (DV) are based on a 2,000 calorie diet.	Vitamin A 170% • Vitamin C 45% • Calcium 10% • Iron 20%			

FETA SPINACH CHICKEN SAUSAGE WITH VEGGIES

SERVES ABOUT 1 ½

1) 3 TBSP Sunflower Oil
2) ¼ C. Vegetable Broth
3) 2 Cloves of Garlic (chopped)
4) 1 Vidalia Onion or Shallot (chopped)
5) ¼ C. Yellow and Green Peppers (diced)
6) Dash of Curry Powder
7) 4 oz. Feta Spinach Chicken Sausage (de-cased)
8) Salt and Pepper, to taste
9) 4 Leaves Swiss Chard (finely chopped)
10) 1 tsp Extra Virgin Olive Oil

In a hot skillet, sauté ingredients 1-6. Cover and cook for four minutes. Add sausage to the skillet and cook for three more minutes. Add salt and pepper and rest the chard on top of sausage. Allow the greens to wilt; it should take about one minute. Then, fold all ingredients together. To finish, drizzle with your favorite extra virgin olive oil.

Eat this ~ You will drastically lower the sodium in this dish if you use half the sausage and substitute lean turkey in its place.

Nutrition Facts	Amount/serving	%DV*	Amount/serving	%DV*
Serv. Size 6 oz (170g)	**Total Fat** 12g	**18%**	**Total Carb.** 7g	**2%**
Calories 160	Sat. Fat 3.5g	**18%**	Fiber 2g	**8%**
Fat Cal. 110	*Trans* Fat 0g		Sugars 2g	
	Cholest. 25mg	**8%**	**Protein** 8g	
	Sodium 370mg	**15%**		
*Percent Daily Values (DV) are based on a 2,000 calorie diet.	Vitamin A 80% • Vitamin C 100% • Calcium 6% • Iron 10%			

10 Minutes

10 Minutes

SAUTÉED FILET MIGNON WITH PEPPERY PARSNIPS

SERVES ABOUT 1 ½

1) 1 TBSP Sunflower Oil
2) 1 Clove of Garlic (diced)
3) 1 Small Spanish Onion (sliced)
4) 3 Parsnips (peeled and thinly sliced on mandolin)
5) ⅓ C. Vegetable Broth
6) Dash of Salt and Fresh Pepper
7) 1 TBSP Butter
8) 5 oz. Filet Mignon (¾-inch thick)
9) Handful of Baby Spinach
10) 6 Red Peppercorns

In a medium to hot skillet, heat sunflower oil. Combine ingredients 2-4 in skillet and sauté for two minutes. Add ingredients 5-7 and cook for one minute. Rest filet in skillet and cook each side for two to three minutes or until it reaches an internal temperature of 155 degrees. Right before the filet is done, add in the spinach - it will wilt quickly. You should have more broth or butter on reserve if moisture is needed to keep the meat from burning. To plate: rest filet on top of all the ingredients. To finish, garnish with red peppercorns. For a nice presentation, rest chives on top.

Eat this in the sun ~ Sunflower oil is packed with vitamin E and is low in saturated fat. Garlic is rich in protein, vitamin A, B, C, iron, calcium and selenium. Onions have just enough dietary fiber and vitamin C to meet the entire day's nutritional requirements. Your filet mignon has an arsenal of vitamins B-6 and B-12 so chew it slowly, don't just swallow it. Lastly, the parsnips are pumped with vitamin C, calcium and iron; they are also a healthy alternative to the Idaho potato. If you eat this dish in the sun – you'll have your vitamin D!

Nutrition Facts	Amount/serving	%DV*	Amount/serving	%DV*
Serv. Size 6 oz (170g)	Total Fat 20g	30%	Total Carb. 11g	4%
Calories 290	Sat. Fat 7g	34%	Fiber 3g	13%
Fat Cal. 170	Trans Fat 0g		Sugars 3g	
	Cholest. 65mg	21%	Protein 18g	
	Sodium 85mg	4%		
*Percent Daily Values (DV) are based on a 2,000 calorie diet.	Vitamin A 70% • Vitamin C 35% • Calcium 6% • Iron 20%			

TURKEY SAUSAGE WITH COLLARD GREENS

SERVES ABOUT 1 ½

1) 2 TBSP Sunflower Oil
2) 1 Spanish Onion (diced)
3) 1 Clove of Garlic (diced)
4) 8 oz. Turkey Sausage (de-cased)
5) Dash of Dulse Flakes or Sea Seasoning of your choice
6) ⅓ C. Vegetable Broth
7) 6 Cherry Tomatoes (cut in ½)
8) Dash of Cinnamon
9) 2 Collard Green Leaves

Turkey sausage has substantially less sodium than pork sausage, making this recipe considerably healthier. In a hot skillet, sauté ingredients 1–7. As the turkey sausage is cooking, break it apart with a rubber spatula. Cook for three minutes or until sausage cooks thoroughly. Cut collard greens into small pieces then rest in skillet and cover for two minutes. Garnish with a dash of cinnamon. Serve this with a side dish or grab a pita, taco, or gluten-free wrap and roll it up.

To make it toasty ~ Toast a roll and spread maple chipotle mustard inside. If you happen to have cilantro, chop up 1 TBSP and add to toasted roll. Complete the sandwich by adding your turkey sausage and collard greens. You can't mess this up!

Nutrition Facts	Amount/serving	%DV*	Amount/serving	%DV*
Serv. Size 6 oz (170g)	Total Fat 21g	33%	Total Carb. 3g	1%
Calories 310	Sat. Fat 4g	20%	Fiber 1g	4%
Fat Cal. 190	*Trans* Fat 0g		Sugars 0g	
	Cholest. 70mg	24%	Protein 25g	
	Sodium 80mg	3%		
*Percent Daily Values (DV) are based on a 2,000 calorie diet.	Vitamin A 60% • Vitamin C 15% • Calcium 6% • Iron 10%			

8 Minutes

SIDE DISHES

ASPARAGUS WITH CREAMY STRAWBERRY TOMATOES

CHEESY TOASTED BREAD

CREAMY LEEKS WITH BABY SPINACH

CRUNCHY PISTACHIO BEET SALAD

DYNAMITE EDAMAME

ELEGANT EGGPLANT APPETIZER

FRESH SWEET BASIL WITH RIPE TOMATOES

BASIC HOMEMADE HUMMUS

JAZZED UP POTATO CHIPS

PORT WINE DRIZZLE

SAUTÉED BROCCOLI RABE WITH GARLIC

SHIITAKE BRUSCHETTA WITH VIDALIA ONIONS

SUCCULENT TOMATO SNACK

SWEET PEPPERS WITH SWISS CHARD

CRUNCHY ZUCCHINI WITH ONIONS

10 Minutes

ASPARAGUS WITH CREAMY STRAWBERRY TOMATOES

SERVES ABOUT 2

1) 2 TBSP Sunflower Oil
2) 5 Asparagus Stalks
3) Salt and Pepper, to taste
4) 1 oz. Crumbled Goat Cheese or Gran Queso (grated)
5) 12 Strawberry Candy Tomatoes (cut in half)
6) 1 tsp Villa Manodori Balsamic Vinegar
7) 1 Clove of Garlic (diced and crushed)
8) 1 TBSP Extra Virgin Olive Oil

In a hot skillet, heat sunflower oil. Break off the bottom ends of the asparagus (they will snap off fairly easily). You can even toss these ends in your garden or compost. Sauté and season the asparagus stalks with salt and pepper. Cook in the skillet for three to five minutes until tender, but not mushy. Remove, allow to cool off, and then slice on a 45 degree angle into bite-sized pieces. In a bowl, combine ingredients 5 and 7 and incorporate the asparagus. Then, drizzle with balsamic vinegar and extra virgin olive oil over it. To garnish, use either goat cheese or gran queso to your liking. Believe it or not – cheese contributes to all of the saturated fat in this dish; however it is such a small amount that it doesn't register on my care-o-meter.

Eat this ~ Keep in mind, while white asparagus is very tasty, green asparagus contains many more beneficial nutrients for your body, simply because the white color doesn't contain chlorophyll. White asparagus also doesn't get any sunlight. It is made through a process called etiolation; which simply means to bleach or alter the natural development of a green plant by excluding the beautiful sunlight. This essentially deprives the vegetable of all the minerals and enzymes our bodies need to live.

Nutrition Facts	Amount/serving	%DV*	Amount/serving	%DV*
Serv. Size 6 oz (170g)	Total Fat 16g	24%	Total Carb. 6g	2%
	Sat. Fat 3.5g	17%	Fiber 1g	6%
Calories 180	*Trans* Fat 0g		Sugars 1g	
Fat Cal. 140	Cholest. 5mg	2%	Protein 4g	
	Sodium 70mg	3%		
*Percent Daily Values (DV) are based on a 2,000 calorie diet.	Vitamin A 10% • Vitamin C 30% • Calcium 2% • Iron 4%			

CHEESY TOASTED BREAD

SERVES 2

1) 1 TBSP Sunflower Oil
2) 2 Slices Italian Bread (the crustier, the better)
3) 1 oz. Pecorino Cheese
4) 3 Drops of Aged Balsamic Vinegar
5) 1 TBSP Extra Virgin Olive Oil
6) Dash of Pepper

In a skillet, heat the sunflower oil. While that's heating, remove both ends from a tuna fish can, or any can, and use that to press down on the bread to form about four perfect circles of bread. Place these circles of bread in a hot skillet and toast each side for forty seconds or until golden brown. Remove and sprinkle with ingredients 3-6. It's a simple and easy snack with any beverage and goes perfectly with any meal, hot or cold.

To make it attractive ~ Rest a roasted sweet red pepper on top. Toasting bread in a skillet with oil completely changes the texture of the bread versus cooking it in the toaster, as it leaves the center moist and adds a harder crust. To minimize the salt content, add less pecorino cheese.

Nutrition Facts	Amount/serving	%DV*	Amount/serving	%DV*
Serv. Size 2 oz (57g)	Total Fat 15g	23%	Total Carb. 18g	6%
	Sat. Fat 3.5g	17%	Fiber 0g	0%
Calories 240	Trans Fat 0g		Sugars 0g	
Fat Cal. 130	Cholest. 10mg	3%	Protein 7g	
	Sodium 200mg	8%		
*Percent Daily Values (DV) are based on a 2,000 calorie diet.	Vitamin A 2% • Vitamin C 0%		• Calcium 20% • Iron 6%	

5 Minutes

6 Minutes

CREAMY LEEKS WITH BABY SPINACH

SERVES 3

1) 1 TBSP Sunflower Oil
2) 1 Shallot (minced)
3) 1 Leek Stalk (white portion only, sliced)
4) 1 Shake Curry Powder
5) 2 TBSP Heavy Cream
6) Salt and Pepper, to taste
7) Handful of Baby Spinach
8) ¼ Lemon (juice and zest)

If you've never had leeks before, they have a subtle onion flavor and look like overgrown scallions. The green tops are edible, but not used in this recipe.

In a skillet on high, heat sunflower oil and combine ingredients 2–4. Cook for four minutes. Add ingredients 5-7 and continue to stir, allowing spinach to wilt (it won't take more than ninety seconds). Finish with juice and zest of ¼ of a lemon. The best tool to use for zesting is a Microplane grater.

To make this spectacular ~ For a last minute snack or a late guest, slice a French baguette in ¼ inch pieces, and lightly toast it in your skillet with a tsp of butter until golden brown. Lightly spread this mixture on the toasted baguette and sink your teeth into heaven!

Nutrition Facts

Serv. Size 5 oz (142g)

Calories 110
Fat Cal. 70

Amount/serving	%DV*	Amount/serving	%DV*
Total Fat 8g	13%	Total Carb. 8g	3%
Sat. Fat 2.5g	13%	Fiber 7g	30%
Trans Fat 0g		Sugars 1g	
Cholest. 15mg	4%	Protein 3g	
Sodium 110mg	5%		

*Percent Daily Values (DV) are based on a 2,000 calorie diet.

Vitamin A 15% • Vitamin C 50% • Calcium 10% • Iron 30%

CRUNCHY PISTACHIO BEET SALAD

SERVES 4

1) 2 TBSP Sunflower Oil
2) 1 Small Onion (sliced)
3) 1 Small Red Beet (thinly sliced on mandolin)
4) 1 Clove of Garlic (diced)
5) 1 TBSP Pistachio Nuts
6) 9 Dandelion Leaves (chopped)
7) Pepper, to taste
8) 1 tsp Italian Seasoning
9) 2 Chives (thinly chopped)
10) 1 tsp Extra Virgin Olive Oil

In a hot skillet, heat sunflower oil. Sauté onions for three to five minutes. Then, combine ingredients 3-5 and cook for three minutes. Lastly, rest chopped dandelions on top of mixture in skillet. Add ingredients 7 and 8, then cover and cook for two minutes. Garnish with thinly chopped chives and extra virgin olive oil.

To make this colorful ~ Add lemon zest on top. For an alternative to dandelions, you can substitute with frisée or endives. Frisée is a French word that means curly. It has a slightly bitter flavor but goes very well with hot dishes. Endives are also slightly bitter with very little nutrients, but are easy to eat and provide a nice looking presentation.

Nutrition Facts

Serv. Size 4 oz (113g)
Calories 140
Fat Cal. 90

Amount/serving	%DV*	Amount/serving	%DV*
Total Fat 11g	16%	Total Carb. 10g	3%
Sat. Fat 1g	6%	Fiber 3g	13%
Trans Fat 0g		Sugars 5g	
Cholest. 0mg	0%	Protein 3g	
Sodium 65mg	3%		

*Percent Daily Values (DV) are based on a 2,000 calorie diet.

Vitamin A 60% • Vitamin C 35% • Calcium 10% • Iron 10%

9 Minutes

8 Minutes

DYNAMITE EDAMAME

SERVES 2

1) 2 TBSP Sunflower Oil
2) ½ Onion (diced)
3) ½ C. Frozen Edamame
4) ¼ C. Vegetable Broth
5) 1 Clove of Garlic (diced)
6) 2 TBSP Parsley
7) Salt and Pepper, to taste
8) Pinch Curry Powder
9) ¼ Lemon (juice)

Heat sunflower oil in skillet. Combine ingredients 1-6 and reduce liquid by 50 percent. In other words, cook down the liquid by half. Add ingredients 7-9. You can fold this into any pasta of your choice; fresh semolina pasta is just an idea. Using fresh pasta as opposed to boxed pasta is a great way to save time and eat healthy.

To make it shine ~ Drizzle six drops of infused oil over this dish - basil oil makes for a great choice.

Nutrition Facts	Amount/serving	%DV*	Amount/serving	%DV*
Serv. Size 7 oz (198g)	**Total Fat** 20g	**30%**	**Total Carb.** 15g	**5%**
Calories 270	Sat. Fat 2g	**11%**	Fiber 4g	**17%**
Fat Cal. 170	*Trans* Fat 0g		Sugars 2g	
	Cholest. 0mg	**0%**	**Protein** 13g	
	Sodium 55mg	**2%**		
*Percent Daily Values (DV) are based on a 2,000 calorie diet.	Vitamin A 10% • Vitamin C 60% • Calcium 20% • Iron 20%			

ELEGANT EGGPLANT APPETIZER

SERVES 4

1) 1 Eggplant
2) 4 TBSP Grated Parmigiano Reggiano
3) $\frac{1}{4}$ tsp Extra Virgin Olive Oil
4) $\frac{1}{2}$ Lemon (juice and zest)
5) 2 Bay Leaves
6) 3 Chives (thinly chopped)
7) 5 Kalamata Olives
8) 2 Slices Prosciutto (optional- ask for speck prosciutto)
9) $\frac{1}{4}$ C. Water
10) 1 TBSP Sunflower Oil

Cut off the first two inches of the skinny end of the eggplant. Then, using your mandolin, cut four super-thin slices. In a hot skillet, heat sunflower oil. Add eggplant and toast until golden brown on both sides, adding water to prevent sticking. If you would like, add your favorite seasonings. Oregano, thyme or herbs de provence are all great options. Remove and lay cooked eggplant on a clean cutting board. Place $\frac{1}{2}$ slice of prosciutto on each eggplant. Sprinkle 1 TBSP grated Parmigiano Reggiano cheese on top of each slice. I'm proud to say it only contributes to 1.74g of saturated fat. To finish, sprinkle lemon zest and juice evenly throughout and roll them up.

To plate: Dust your plate with fresh ground pepper (optional), place bay leaves on an angle in center and rest the olives on the side. Garnish with chives and extra virgin olive oil. Then rest the eggplant in the center of the plate.

To make this romantic ~ A simple glass of champagne is a great complement to this appetizer. If you're not a fan of eggplant, remove it and just use the prosciutto as the wrap. Prosciutto is easier to work with at room temperature.

Nutrition Facts	Amount/serving	%DV*	Amount/serving	%DV*
Serv. Size 2 oz (57g)	Total Fat 6g	9%	Total Carb. 3g	1%
Calories 80	Sat. Fat 1.5g	7%	Fiber 2g	6%
Fat Cal. 50	Trans Fat 0g		Sugars 1g	
	Cholest. 10mg	4%	Protein 4g	
	Sodium 250mg	11%		
*Percent Daily Values (DV) are based on a 2,000 calorie diet.	Vitamin A 2% • Vitamin C 8%		• Calcium 4% • Iron 2%	

5 Minutes

10 Minutes

FRESH SWEET BASIL WITH RIPE TOMATOES

SERVES 5

1) 8 Tomatoes (diced)
2) 3 TBSP Infused Olive Oil (O Olive Oil is always a nice choice)
3) 1 Clove of Garlic (minced)
4) 10 Basil Leaves (sliced julienne*)
5) ¼ C. Sliced Almonds
6) 2 Shakes Cayenne Pepper
7) Salt and Pepper, to taste
8) 1 tsp Lemon Zest

Place diced tomatoes in a bowl. Add ingredients 2-7 and garnish with lemon zest. You could use this as a topping or as a garnish for fish. Or you can toss it with brown rice or anything you desire.

To give it a zing ~ Replace the basil with cilantro and finish with toasted bread. You'll find that the more you create your own alternatives, the more you build up your own personality in the kitchen.

* **Note**: To accomplish a julienne cut, stack leaves and cut on an angle into ⅛ inch strips.

Nutrition Facts	Amount/serving	%DV*	Amount/serving	%DV*
Serv. Size 4 oz (113g)	Total Fat 10g	15%	Total Carb. 7g	2%
	Sat. Fat 1g	5%	Fiber 2g	9%
Calories 120	Trans Fat 0g		Sugars 3g	
Fat Cal. 90	Cholest. 0mg	0%	Protein 4g	
	Sodium 15mg	1%		
*Percent Daily Values (DV) are based on a 2,000 calorie diet.	Vitamin A 15% • Vitamin C 35% • Calcium 4% • Iron 8%			

SERVES 9

1) 7 oz Tahini (buy it or make it)
2) 4 Cloves of Garlic
3) 1 TBSP Parsley or Cilantro
4) 1 Can Chickpeas or Garbanzo Beans
5) 1 tsp Extra Virgin Olive Oil
6) 1/3 C. Water
7) 1/2 Lemon (juice and zest)
8) Sea Salt, to taste

In a food processor, combine ingredients 1-7 and pulse for eight seconds. To tailor hummus to your liking, add more water for your desired thickness. Remember, you don't want to break your chip when you dip it! Always taste before adding the sea salt.

To make it festive ~ With this foundation, you could add sautéed onions, lime juice, sun-dried tomatoes, chipotle sauce with peppers, pine nuts, cashews, walnuts, chili powder, cumin, coriander, cayenne pepper, or curry powder. You can even style for certain holidays by adding pumpkin purée or even avocado for a St. Patrick's Day hummus! Go ahead and use your own creativity and ingenuity.

Nutrition Facts Serv. Size 2 oz (57g)	Amount/serving	%DV*	Amount/serving	%DV*
Calories 200	**Total Fat** 11g	17%	**Total Carb.** 20g	7%
Fat Cal. 100	Sat. Fat 1.5g	7%	Fiber 3g	10%
	Trans Fat 0g		Sugars 0g	
	Cholest. 0mg	0%	**Protein** 8g	
	Sodium 35mg	1%		
*Percent Daily Values (DV) are based on a 2,000 calorie diet.	Vitamin A 10% •	Vitamin C 6% •	Calcium 10% •	Iron 15%

10 Minutes

6Minutes

JAZZED UP POTATO CHIPS

SERVES 9

1) 8 oz. Baked Potato Chips (Nana's Cocina is my favorite)
2) ¼ C. Parsley (chopped)
3) ¼ C. Cilantro (chopped)
4) 1 Lime (juice)
5) 1 TBSP Extra Virgin Olive Oil
6) 3 TBSP Crumbled Goat Cheese

I just love this recipe! It's a real treat with basic, healthy ingredients. I prefer chips made from sunflower or peanut oil. In a bowl, combine chips with parsley, cilantro, lime juice and drizzle with extra virgin olive oil. Finish it with crumbles of goat cheese. These are great with a crusty panini!

To dress it up ~ Nothing, just eat 'em up!

Nutrition Facts

Serv. Size 2 oz (57g)
Calories 210
Fat Cal. 60

Amount/serving	%DV*	Amount/serving	%DV*
Total Fat 7g	10%	**Total Carb.** 31g	10%
Sat. Fat 1.5g	8%	Fiber 4g	16%
Trans Fat 0g		Sugars 2g	
Cholest. 0mg	0%	**Protein** 7g	
Sodium 210mg	9%		

*Percent Daily Values (DV) are based on a 2,000 calorie diet.

Vitamin A 8% • Vitamin C 30% • Calcium 8% • Iron 20%

SERVES 4

1) 1 C. Port wine
2) 5 tsp Butter
3) 2 Chives (chopped)

This may very well be the best drizzle for any red meat dish! It can also be used as a decorative finish to a plate. It's a really nice presentation that will impress your guests.

On medium to high heat, combine 1 C. Port wine and reduce by 50%. In other words, cook down the liquid by half. Then, add 1 tsp butter. Repeat this step until it thickens; adding one tsp of butter at a time. Wait until each piece of butter melts before adding the next. Once the sauce reduces, add very finely chopped chives for an amazing finish!

To make it sweeter ~ You can use any dessert wine, such as Sauternes, which is from a region in France.

Nutrition Facts	Amount/serving	%DV*	Amount/serving	%DV*
Serv. Size 1 oz (28g)	Total Fat 2g	3%	Total Carb. 1g	0%
Calories 40	Sat. Fat 1.5g	7%	Fiber 0g	0%
Fat Cal. 20	*Trans* Fat 0g		Sugars 0g	
	Cholest. 5mg	2%	**Protein** 0g	
	Sodium 0mg	0%		
*Percent Daily Values (DV) are based on a 2,000 calorie diet.	Vitamin A 2% • Vitamin C 0% • Calcium 0% • Iron 0%			

10 Minutes

7 Minutes

SERVES 3

1) 1 TBSP Sunflower Oil
2) ¼ C. Sliced Almonds
3) Bunch of Broccoli Rabe
4) ¼ Lemon (juice)
5) 3 Cloves of Garlic (crushed)
6) ⅓ C. Vegetable Broth
7) 1 TBSP Extra Virgin Olive Oil

Chop off ½ inch from the ends of the broccoli rabe. With your knife, make a cross on the bottom of the stem to allow flavors to penetrate through. In a moderately heated skillet, heat sunflower oil and sauté garlic for two minutes. Add almonds and broth, then allow it to reduce for two minutes. Incorporate broccoli rabe and cook for four more minutes. Finish by squeezing in lemon juice and adding extra virgin olive oil.

To complement this dish ~ This lends itself well to penne pasta, linguine or you can make a sandwich by toasting a French baguette. Add a few crushed olives and you'll love it!

Nutrition Facts	Amount/serving	%DV*	Amount/serving	%DV*
Serv. Size 4 oz (113g)	Total Fat 14g	21%	Total Carb. 6g	2%
Calories 160	Sat. Fat 1.5g	7%	Fiber 3g	13%
Fat Cal. 120	*Trans* Fat 0g		Sugars 1g	
	Cholest. 0mg	0%	Protein 5g	
	Sodium 45mg	2%		
*Percent Daily Values (DV) are based on a 2,000 calorie diet.	Vitamin A 60% • Vitamin C 50% • Calcium 10% • Iron 8%			

SHIITAKE BRUSCHETTA WITH VIDALIA ONIONS

SERVES 4

1) 1 French Loaf Baguette (sliced ½ inch thick on a 45 degree angle)
2) 10 Shiitake Mushrooms (sliced)
3) 1 Vidalia Onion (thinly sliced)
4) 1 TBSP Butter
5) Seasonings, to taste (go for it – choose your own!)
6) ½ Lemon (juice and zest)
7) ¼ C. Pecorino Cheese

In a hot skillet, melt half the butter. Add onions and cook for two minutes. Combine mushrooms with lemon zest and juice and cook for five more minutes. Remove mixture from skillet and place on reserve. Sprinkle seasonings on the slices of bread. In the same skillet, melt the remaining butter, add the sliced bread and toast until desired color. I like it to be golden brown. Top bread with mushroom mixture and sprinkle with pecorino cheese. Note: In this recipe most of the sodium is coming from the bread.

To make it special ~ Drizzle with extra virgin olive oil and red pepper flakes.

Nutrition Facts	Amount/serving	%DV*	Amount/serving	%DV*
Serv. Size 3 oz (85g)	Total Fat 8g	12%	Total Carb. 22g	7%
	Sat. Fat 2g	9%	Fiber 1g	4%
Calories 170	Trans Fat 0g		Sugars 1g	
Fat Cal. 70	Cholest. 5mg	2%	Protein 4g	
	Sodium 380mg	16%		
*Percent Daily Values (DV) are based on a 2,000 calorie diet.	Vitamin A 2% • Vitamin C 10% • Calcium 4% • Iron 2%			

9 Minutes

9 Minutes

SUCCULENT TOMATO SNACK

SERVES 12

1) 20 Cherry tomatoes (cut in half)
2) 4 TBSP Extra Virgin Olive Oil
3) Salt and Pepper, to taste
4) ¼ C. Gruyere Cheese (cubed)
5) 2 Shakes Curry Powder or Cayenne Pepper
6) 1 Clove of Garlic (minced)
7) 1 tsp Villa Manodori Balsamic Vinegar
8) ½ tsp Thyme (fresh or dried)

In a bowl, combine all ingredients and toss well. You could do almost anything to this simple dish, such as adding it to pasta, steak tips, rice, leftover chicken or smoked salmon. Whole Foods Market has a terrific selection of smokin' smoked salmon, which they do in-house. Try it with this snack!

To make this amazing ~ Try this with aged gouda and drops of lemon juice.

Nutrition Facts	Amount/serving	%DV*	Amount/serving	%DV*
Serv. Size 4 oz (113g)	Total Fat 6g	10%	Total Carb. 4g	1%
	Sat. Fat 1.5g	8%	Fiber 1g	5%
Calories 80	Trans Fat 0g		Sugars 3g	
Fat Cal. 50	Cholest. 5mg	2%	Protein 2g	
	Sodium 25mg	1%		
*Percent Daily Values (DV) are based on a 2,000 calorie diet.	Vitamin A 20% • Vitamin C 20% • Calcium 6% • Iron 2%			

SWEET PEPPERS WITH SWISS CHARD

SERVES 7

1) 2 TBSP Sunflower Oil
2) 2 Cloves of Garlic (minced)
3) 1 Vidalia Onion or Shallot (thinly chopped)
4) ¼ C. Yellow and Red Peppers (diced)
5) 1 Shake Cayenne Pepper
6) Salt and Pepper, to taste
7) 4 Large Leaves Swiss Chard (red or green, finely chopped)
8) 1 TBSP Extra Virgin Olive Oil

In a hot skillet, heat sunflower oil and sauté ingredients 2-5. Cook for four minutes. Add salt and pepper to taste, then rest the chard in skillet. Allow it to wilt for about three minutes. Stir and fold in all ingredients. To finish: drizzle with extra virgin olive oil.

To make this juicy ~ Combine Feta Spinach Chicken Sausage with vidalia onions. Cook for an additional three minutes. By de-casing sausage, you will add flavor to the dish - not to mention that it will speed up the cooking process! By adding meat, the total fat, cholesterol and sodium will increase – so eaters beware!

Nutrition Facts	Amount/serving	%DV*	Amount/serving	%DV*
Serv. Size 3 oz (85g)	**Total Fat** 9g	14%	**Total Carb.** 3g	1%
Calories 110	**Sat.** Fat 2g	10%	Fiber 1g	4%
Fat Cal. 80	*Trans* Fat 0g		Sugars 1g	
	Cholest. 15mg	5%	**Protein** 5g	
	Sodium 300mg	13%		
*Percent Daily Values (DV) are based on a 2,000 calorie diet.	Vitamin A 40% • Vitamin C 35% • Calcium 2% • Iron 6%			

10 Minutes

10 Minutes

CRUNCHY ZUCCHINI WITH ONIONS

SERVES 2

1) 1 TBSP Sunflower Oil
2) 1 Large Zucchini (sliced on mandolin)
3) 1 Spanish Onion (sliced on mandolin)
4) 1 TBSP Capers
5) Dash of All-Purpose Spike Seasoning
6) Pepper, to taste
7) 2 tsp Butter
8) 5 Cashew Nuts
9) 2 Leaves Marjoram or Mint

In a hot skillet, heat sunflower oil and sauté zucchini for three minutes Add ingredients 3-7. Cook for four to five minutes. Toss in cashews, stir, then remove from heat. Garnish with mint or marjoram. You can add this to almost anything, such as a last-minute topping on some crusty Tuscan bread, as filling for a stuffed filet of sole, or fill and roll with your favorite cheese.

To make this crazy healthy ~ Remember you can also throw in some Sea Seasonings - conveniently found in the spice section at Whole Foods Market. You can easily use this side dish in a wrap or on a taco and garnish with cilantro.

Nutrition Facts

Serv. Size 7 oz (198g)

Calories 120

Fat Cal. 80

Amount/serving	%DV*	Amount/serving	%DV*
Total Fat 9g	15%	Total Carb. 10g	3%
Sat. Fat 3g	14%	Fiber 2g	9%
Trans Fat 0g		Sugars 4g	
Cholest. 10mg	3%	Protein 2g	
Sodium 55mg	2%		

*Percent Daily Values (DV) are based on a 2,000 calorie diet.

Vitamin A 8% • Vitamin C 45% • Calcium 4% • Iron 4%

DESSERTS

APPLE SAUCE

BANANA BOAT WITH SPICED BLUEBERRY PUREE

ICE COLD WATERMELON WITH LEMON JUICE

MANGO TANGO DESSERT

PINEAPPLE SPILT WITH MEYER LEMONS

HONEY FIGS WITH PINEAPPLE AND MANGO PURÉE

SMOOTH AND SWEET BLUEBERRY PUDDING

SOUR APPLE TREAT

SWEET MINTY TRIO

VERY BERRY DELIGHT

WARM APPLE BANANA DESSERT

10 Minutes

APPLE SAUCE

SERVES 8

1) 1 C. Water
2) 2 Granny Smith Apples (peeled and sliced)
3) 2 TBSP Honey or Agave Nectar
4) ¼ tsp Cinnamon
5) Dash of Nutmeg
6) ¼ Lemon (juice)
7) 1 Orange (juice and zest)
8) 3 Raspberries

On high heat, place apples in skillet, add enough water to cover apples and cook for two minutes. Add ingredients 3-6 and cook for six minutes. Remove from heat. Place in food processor and pulse for five seconds. Finish with orange zest and juice. Garnish with raspberries for a little color.

To make it sweet and chewy ~ Add a handful of golden delicious raisins or cacao powder.

Nutrition Facts	Amount/serving	%DV*	Amount/serving	%DV*
Serv. Size 5 oz (142g)	Total Fat 0.5g	1%	Total Carb. 18g	6%
	Sat. Fat 0g	0%	Fiber 2g	8%
Calories 60	Trans Fat 0g		Sugars 15g	
Fat Cal. 5	Cholest. 0mg	0%	Protein 0g	
	Sodium 0mg	0%		
*Percent Daily Values (DV) are based on a 2,000 calorie diet.	Vitamin A 0% • Vitamin C 15% • Calcium 2% • Iron 0%			

BANANA BOAT WITH SPICED BLUEBERRY PUREE

SERVES 7

1) 2 Bananas
2) ¼ Lemon
3) Handful of Blueberries
4) Dash of Clove Powder
5) ⅓ C. Blueberry or Grape Juice
6) 4 Ice Cubes
7) 2 TBSP Cacao Nibs

In a blender or food processor, add 1 banana and combine ingredients 2-6 ice cubes. Puree for eight seconds. Slice other banana into small pieces and stack in the center of a dish. Pour puréed mixture over top and garnish with cacao nibs. If you need more liquid, add 1 to 2 oz. of water or coconut water. You can also garnish with crushed gluten-free quinoa cookies, or any cookie, for that matter.

To make this bee-licious ~ Add Manuka honey to the purée.

Nutrition Facts	Amount/serving	%DV*	Amount/serving	%DV*
Serv. Size 4 oz (113g)	Total Fat 2.5g	3%	Total Carb. 27g	9%
	Sat. Fat 1.5g	7%	Fiber 5g	19%
Calories 120	Trans Fat 0g		Sugars 18g	
Fat Cal. 20	Cholest. 0mg	0%	Protein 1g	
	Sodium 5mg	0%		
*Percent Daily Values (DV) are based on a 2,000 calorie diet.	Vitamin A 0% • Vitamin C 70% • Calcium 4% • Iron 4%			

6 Minutes

4 Minutes

ICE COLD WATERMELON WITH LEMON JUICE

SERVES 3

1) 12 oz. Watermelon
2) 1 Lemon (juice and zest)
3) 1 Lime (juice and zest)

This treat is refreshing and extremely alkalizing. Alkalizing foods aid in the prevention of illness by balancing your pH levels. Slice watermelon into bite-sized pieces and place in a bowl. Sprinkle with the juice and zest of the lemon and lime.

To make it minty ~ Chop a handful of mint, spearmint or peppermint and sprinkle on top of watermelon. To give it a chill, place melon in the freezer for six minutes before serving.

Nutrition Facts	Amount/serving	%DV*	Amount/serving	%DV*
Serv. Size 6 oz (170g)	Total Fat 0g	0%	Total Carb. 13g	4%
	Sat. Fat 0g	0%	Fiber 1g	3%
Calories 50	Trans Fat 0g		Sugars 10g	
Fat Cal. 0	Cholest. 0mg	0%	Protein 1g	
	Sodium 0mg	0%		
*Percent Daily Values (DV) are based on a 2,000 calorie diet.	Vitamin A 15% • Vitamin C 40% • Calcium 2% • Iron 2%			

SERVES 4

1) 2 Ripe Mangoes
2) ½ Lime (juice and zest)
3) 5 Strawberries (remove greens)
4) 1 tsp Cinnamon
5) ½ C. Mango Juice

Amazingly dee-licious and alkalizing. Remove skin and stone from mangoes. Slice into cubes and place in bowl. Purée ingredients 3-5 in food processor or blender. To plate: place mango cubes in center and drizzle with strawberry purée. Lastly, dice zest of lime. Shower plate with lime juice and zest.

Eat this ~ Ideal mangoes are red and yellow. The ones that have the most red are the ripest because they were exposed to greater amounts of sunlight. Yellow = limited light. Green = shade.

Nutrition Facts	Amount/serving	%DV*	Amount/serving	%DV*
Serv. Size 4 oz (113g)	Total Fat 0g	0%	Total Carb. 15g	5%
Calories 60	Sat. Fat 0g	0%	Fiber 2g	7%
Fat Cal. 0	Trans Fat 0g		Sugars 13g	
	Cholest. 0mg	0%	Protein 1g	
	Sodium 0mg	0%		
*Percent Daily Values (DV) are based on a 2,000 calorie diet.	Vitamin A 10% • Vitamin C 70% • Calcium 2% • Iron 2%			

6
Minutes

6 Minutes

SERVES 2

1) ¾ C. Pineapple Chunks
2) 1 TBSP Lemon Sorbet
3) 1 Orange (zest and juice)
4) 1 Meyer Lemon (zest and juice)
5) Sprig of Cilantro

Place pineapple chunks in a bowl. Juice lemon and orange over the pineapple. Garnish with preferred amount of zest from each fruit. Place sorbet on top. Finish with a sprig of cilantro.

Eat this ~ Meyer lemons have a rounder shape and smoother skin than common commercial lemons; their color ranges from deep yellow to yellow-orange.

Nutrition Facts	Amount/serving	%DV*	Amount/serving	%DV*
Serv. Size 6 oz (170g)	Total Fat 0g	0%	Total Carb. 22g	7%
	Sat. Fat 0g	0%	Fiber 1g	4%
Calories 90	Trans Fat 0g		Sugars 2g	
Fat Cal. 0	Cholest. 0mg	0%	Protein 1g	
	Sodium 5mg	0%		
*Percent Daily Values (DV) are based on a 2,000 calorie diet.	Vitamin A 4% • Vitamin C 50% • Calcium 2% • Iron 2%			

HONEY FIGS WITH PINEAPPLE AND MANGO PURÉE

SERVES 6

1) 1 tsp Manuka Honey
2) 1 tsp Pure Maple Syrup (Grade B - it's a bit thicker)
3) 8 Figs
4) 1 Vanilla Bean
5) ¼ Lemon (juice and zest)
6) 5 Pineapple Chunks
7) ⅓ C. Mango Juice

In your skillet, heat Manuka honey with maple syrup. Pierce the skin of the vanilla bean and remove the vanilla from bean. It will be a small amount, but it will go a long way. Add the vanilla and the lemon juice to the skillet and cook for three minutes. Slice figs into quarters and add to skillet. Cook for an additional three minutes. In the meantime, place pineapple chunks and mango juice into food processor. Pulse for four seconds. To finish, in a bowl, stack figs on a bed of pineapple and mango purée. Garnish with lemon zest. Even if you try to mess this up, you won't! This dessert will still come out perfectly.

Eat this ~ Figs, most noted for their sweetness and soft texture, have a mushy, gushy interior filled with edible seeds. Figs have the shortest life span of any fruit and are a great substitute for sugar in cooking.

Nutrition Facts	Amount/serving	%DV*	Amount/serving	%DV*
Serv. Size 6 oz (170g)	Total Fat 0g	0%	Total Carb. 26g	9%
Calories 100	Sat. Fat 0g	0%	Fiber 2g	8%
Fat Cal. 0	Trans Fat 0g		Sugars 20g	
	Cholest. 0mg	0%	Protein 1g	
	Sodium 0mg	0%		
*Percent Daily Values (DV) are based on a 2,000 calorie diet.	Vitamin A 4% • Vitamin C 40% • Calcium 4% • Iron 2%			

9
Minutes

SERVES 2

1) 1 C. Blueberries
2) 1 tsp Lime or Lemon (juice)
3) Dash of Cinnamon
4) 1 tsp Manuka Honey
5) 1 tsp Arrowroot
6) 1 Strawberry
7) 1 TBSP Pine nuts

This is very easy and a fantastic way to impress your puddin'. In your food processor, combine ingredients 1-3 and pulse for four seconds. Remove and transfer to heated skillet and combine Manuka honey. Add arrowroot incrementally until mixture thickens. Garnish with pine nuts and strawberry. This can be served cold or slightly warmed.

Eat this ~ Blueberries are the Rocky Marciano of fruit. They are undefeated in knocking out and destroying free radicals. They keep you fresh, fit, razor sharp, and in high spirits. They area also very high in vitamin C - and remember the deeper the blue the more healthy in antioxidants.

Nutrition Facts	Amount/serving	%DV*	Amount/serving	%DV*
Serv. Size 5 oz (142g)	Total Fat 1g	1%	Total Carb. 19g	6%
Calories 90	Sat. Fat 0g	0%	Fiber 6g	24%
Fat Cal. 10	*Trans* Fat 0g		Sugars 3g	
	Cholest. 0mg	0%	Protein 1g	
	Sodium 0mg	0%		
*Percent Daily Values (DV) are based on a 2,000 calorie diet.	Vitamin A 4% • Vitamin C 30% • Calcium 2% • Iron 2%			

SERVES ABOUT 5

1) 2 Granny Smith Apples (peeled and sliced)
2) 2 TBSP Agave Nectar
3) $\frac{1}{4}$ Lemon (juice)
4) $\frac{1}{4}$ tsp Cinnamon
5) $\frac{1}{4}$ tsp Clove Powder
6) $\frac{1}{4}$ Orange (juice and zest)
7) $\frac{1}{4}$ tsp Vanilla Powder
8) 2 Cinnamon Sticks

In a bowl, toss ingredients 1 and 2. Add ingredients 3–6. Be sure to zest the orange before squeezing the juice out of it. To remove the zest from orange, use your grater - it's that simple! Garnish with vanilla powder and cinnamon sticks.

Nutrition Facts	Amount/serving	%DV*	Amount/serving	%DV*
Serv. Size 4 oz (113g)	Total Fat 0.5g	1%	Total Carb. 23g	8%
Calories 80	Sat. Fat 0g	0%	Fiber 3g	10%
Fat Cal. 5	Trans Fat 0g		Sugars 20g	
	Cholest. 0mg	0%	Protein 0g	
	Sodium 0mg	0%		
*Percent Daily Values (DV) are based on a 2,000 calorie diet.	Vitamin A 0% • Vitamin C 8% • Calcium 0% • Iron 0%			

9 Minutes

SERVES 3

1) ½ C. Papaya (cubed)
2) ½ C. Honey Dew Melon (cubed)
3) ½ C. Cantaloupe (cubed)
4) 1 Orange (juice and zest)
5) 4 Mint Leaves
6) 1 TBSP Honey
7) 1 TBSP Pure Maple Syrup

Place ingredients 1-3 in a bowl. In a skillet, heat orange juice, zest, honey and syrup for three minutes. Drizzle sauce over fruit and toss. Garnish with mint leaves.

To make it funky ~ Top off this dessert trio with a scoop of crème fraîche or sorbet and serve it with a chilled glass of dessert wine.

Nutrition Facts	Amount/serving	%DV*	Amount/serving	%DV*
Serv. Size 5 oz (142g)	Total Fat 0g	0%	Total Carb. 21g	7%
Calories 80	Sat. Fat 0g	0%	Fiber 3g	12%
Fat Cal. 0	Trans Fat 0g		Sugars 16g	
	Cholest. 0mg	0%	Protein 1g	
	Sodium 15mg	1%		
*Percent Daily Values (DV) are based on a 2,000 calorie diet.	Vitamin A 25% • Vitamin C 80% • Calcium 6% • Iron 8%			

SERVES 3

1) 1 Orange (juice and zest)
2) 1 tsp Rapadura
3) 6 Strawberries (remove greens and slice thinly)
4) ¼ C. Blueberries
5) ¼ C. Seedless Green Grapes

In a bowl, combine orange zest, juice and rapadura. Mix well. Incorporate ingredients 3-5 and toss.

To make it tipsy ~ Add 3 oz. of Grand Marnier to the mixture. Of course, for a much healthier choice, try agave nectar.

Eat this ~ You betcha, strawberries are packed with vitamin C and are berry good for your heart! Many think the strawberry is the only fruit with its seeds on the outside. However, I'm not so sure about that. We might want to ask a pineapple!

Nutrition Facts	Amount/serving	%DV*	Amount/serving	%DV*
Serv. Size 4 oz (113g)	Total Fat 0g	0%	Total Carb. 16g	5%
	Sat. Fat 0g	0%	Fiber 3g	14%
Calories 70	Trans Fat 0g		Sugars 8g	
Fat Cal. 0	Cholest. 0mg	0%	Protein 1g	
	Sodium 0mg	0%		
*Percent Daily Values (DV) are based on a 2,000 calorie diet.	Vitamin A 2% • Vitamin C 60% • Calcium 2% • Iron 2%			

6 Minutes

6Minutes

SERVES 4

1) 1 tsp Agave Nectar
2) 1 Red Delicious Apple (peeled and cubed)
3) 2 Bananas (sliced on an angle)
4) ½ tsp Vanilla Powder or Vanilla Bean
5) 9 Fresh Raspberries
6) 1 Mint Leaf (cut julienne)
7) 1 tsp Orange Zest
8) 1 TBSP Sliced Hazelnuts or Almonds

In a hot skillet, cook apple with agave nectar for four minutes. Add ingredients 3 and 4 and cook for an additional minute. Place mixture in a bowl and top with raspberries. Garnish with nuts, mint and orange zest.

To make it dreamy ~ Lightly dust cacao powder over the top.

Nutrition Facts	Amount/serving	%DV*	Amount/serving	%DV*
Serv. Size 4 oz (113g)	Total Fat 3g	4%	Total Carb. 22g	7%
	Sat. Fat 0g	0%	Fiber 4g	15%
Calories 110	Trans Fat 0g		Sugars 6g	
Fat Cal. 25	Cholest. 0mg	0%	Protein 1g	
	Sodium 0mg	0%		
*Percent Daily Values (DV) are based on a 2,000 calorie diet.	Vitamin A 15% • Vitamin C 15% • Calcium 2% • Iron 4%			

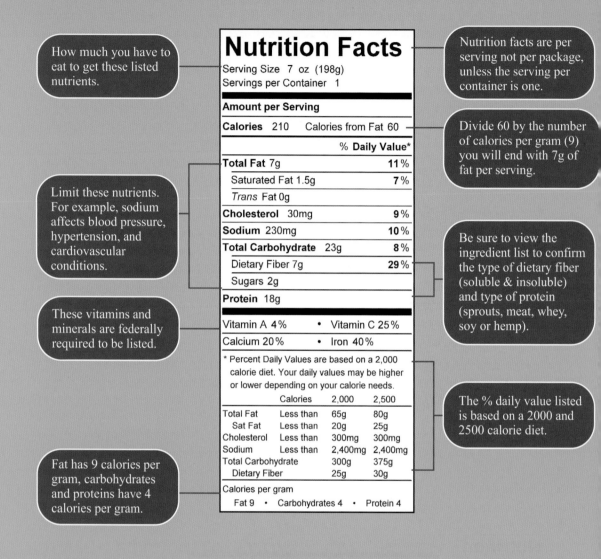

How much you have to eat to get these listed nutrients.

Nutrition facts are per serving not per package, unless the serving per container is one.

Limit these nutrients. For example, sodium affects blood pressure, hypertension, and cardiovascular conditions.

Divide 60 by the number of calories per gram (9) you will end with 7g of fat per serving.

These vitamins and minerals are federally required to be listed.

Be sure to view the ingredient list to confirm the type of dietary fiber (soluble & insoluble) and type of protein (sprouts, meat, whey, soy or hemp).

Fat has 9 calories per gram, carbohydrates and proteins have 4 calories per gram.

The % daily value listed is based on a 2000 and 2500 calorie diet.

Nutrition Facts

Serving Size 7 oz (198g)
Servings per Container 1

Amount per Serving

Calories 210   Calories from Fat 60

% **Daily Value***

Total Fat 7g	**11**%
Saturated Fat 1.5g	**7**%
Trans Fat 0g	
Cholesterol 30mg	**9**%
Sodium 230mg	**10**%
Total Carbohydrate 23g	**8**%
Dietary Fiber 7g	**29**%
Sugars 2g	
Protein 18g	

Vitamin A 4%   •   Vitamin C 25%

Calcium 20%   •   Iron 40%

* Percent Daily Values are based on a 2,000 calorie diet. Your daily values may be higher or lower depending on your calorie needs.

		Calories	2,000	2,500
Total Fat	Less than		65g	80g
Sat Fat	Less than		20g	25g
Cholesterol	Less than		300mg	300mg
Sodium	Less than		2,400mg	2,400mg
Total Carbohydrate			300g	375g
Dietary Fiber			25g	30g

Calories per gram
  Fat 9   •   Carbohydrates 4   •   Protein 4

By eating foods mostly composed of carbohydrates and proteins, you will likely consume fewer calories. If the food contains seeds, sprouts, nuts, grains and oils they tend to be richer in calories, but will give the body more important nutrients. Take a good look at the nutrition facts in addition to the ingredient list! It can and will give you information you need to make changes towards being a healthier you.

ACKNOWLEDGEMENTS

I would like to express my deepest appreciation to my **Mom, Dad** and **Grandparents James & Gina Diaferia and Frank & Jennie Polito**. We are nothing without our lineage and those who gave up comfort so that we would be comfortable.

Gino Diaferia, the greatest uncle in the world. Thanks for giving me the opportunity to work in your restaurant, which to me, is the finest restaurant in America - Veritas, and that's the truth!

To my brother and photographer, **Michael Polito** and his wife **Tammy**. Thank you for giving me your attention, input, effort and the most precious gift of all, of which you have so little, your time.

To my two sisters, **Annmarie** and **Lisa**, with whom I've shared so many unforgettable family meals, you've taught me so much about the importance of family.

To my dear family, friends, co-workers and patrons at **Veritas, Troquet** and **Whole Foods Market**. I'm so rich and thankful to have you as engineers and architects in my life. I'm truly the luckiest man alive. I'm always learning and always improving and at this current rate, I'll be awesome when I'm 90!

A special whole-hearted thanks and appreciation to Catherine Amilcare, Mike & Paula Barone, Tony & Maria Balbo, Chef Andrea Beaman, Chef Scott Bryan, Jean Caputi, Andrea Davis, Rebecca Doherty, Conklin Delphine, Chef Matt Connors, Michael De Marco, Peter Diaferia, Dorthy Dulin, Even Ewing, Mary Fitzgerald, Angelina Fowx, The Furlong Family, Bryan Golden, Jessica Guidoboni, The Hamel Family, Chef Scott Hebert, Trisha Helen, Tim Hulse, Kelly Jackson, Dr. Andrea James, Helen Matthew-Emde, Cathina Kleen, John & Stephanie Mulcahey, Robin Nadeau, Nelson Ruiz, Mary O'Day, Cheryl & David Oppenheim, Kevin Paige, Lisa Reger, Kevin Ruttan, Liz Simpson, Jim Schlipmann, Alex Schmutterer, Maria Sheehan, Pirjo Silen, David Sterling, Lou Strippoli, Jeanne Sylvester, Lindsay Taub, Al & Sue Waters, Carlos Vega, and my love Maricruz for being the inspiration end key ingredient to the recipe of My Life. With all I have and it's a lot, thank you for your constant encouragement and wisdom when it was desperately needed.

To Contact **Tony Polito**
tony@cookingwithtony.com

Photography by: **Michael Polito**
www.michaelpolito.com

Designed by: **Carlos Vega**
AJRoss Creative Media | www.ajross.com

Agave Nectar 50, 173
Alfalfa Sprouts.............75
Almonds.....................55, 56, 68,
100, 153,
161, 193
Apple 173, 168,
193
Apple Cider Vinegar......60, 63, 64,
131
Apricot Juice 39
Arrowroot 127, 185
Arugula Leaves 80
Asparagus 141
Avocado 20, 45, 55,
67, 75,
92,154
Balsamic Vinegar 165
Banana 174, 193
Basil.......................45, 46, 63,
149, 153
Bay Leaves 150
Beans
- Adzuki 68
- Black 46
- Cacao 36
- Cannellini 46
- Edamame 119
- Garbanzo.................46, 67, 84,
154
- Kidney 46
- Soy 46
- Termis 55, 67
Black Pepper 55, 60
Blueberries 35, 36, 50,
68, 174,
185, 190
Boneless Pork Loin.......127
Broccoli....................105, 107,
161
Brown Rice..................153
Buckwheat...................63
Burdock Root 60, 100
Butternut Squash 56, 99,
100, 107
Cabbage 63
Cacao Powder...............173, 193
Cacao Nibs..................29, 36,
174
Cantaloupe 189
Capers 67, 111,
128, 131,
169
Carob Soy Milk.............35, 36
Carrots.....................60
Cashews.....................56, 59, 68,
103, 120,
154, 169
Cayenne Pepper.............25, 30, 35,
39, 46, 55,
60, 100,
131 153,
154, 165,
166
Celery 49

Cheese
- American..................92
- Buffalo Mozzarella....79
- Cheddar 75, 76
- Feta 132, 166
- Goat 60, 75, 83,
141, 157
- Gouda 123, 165
- Gran Queso...............141
- Gruyere 80, 87,
165
- Manchego.................95
- Mozzarella...............79, 92
- Parmesan.................67, 107
- Parmigiano...............99, 150
- Pecorino 142, 162
- Provolone 76
- Ricotta..................119
- Vegan....................87
Chicken 46, 64, 95,
127, 128,
132, 165,
166
Chicken Broth 45, 100
Chicken Stock.............45
Chickpeas 46, 55, 67,
84, 154
Chipotle Mustard 136
Chipotle Sauce............107, 128,
154
Chives 25, 55, 76,
107, 115,
135, 146,
150, 158
Chocolate 29
Cilantro....................25, 45, 59,
63, 84, 91,
92, 136,
153, 154,
157, 169,
181
Cinnamon 35, 39, 50,
136, 173,
178, 185,
186
Cinnamon Sticks 186
Clove Powder...............30, 50,
174, 186
Coconut Wate 174
Collard Greens 136
Concord Grape Juice....35
Coriander 45, 83,
154
Corn 59, 64,
111
Corn Chips..................59, 60, 75
Cream Cheese...............50
Cucumber 76
Cumin 45, 83,
154
Curry Powder...............45, 46, 64,
71, 83, 99,
100, 108,
123, 128,
132, 145,
149, 154,
165

Dandelions 64, 146
Dessert Wine...............158, 189
Dijon Mustard 71
Dill 56, 71
Edamame 45, 119,
149
Eggplant 80, 150
Etiolation 141
Fennel 59
Figs........................182
Filet Mignon 135
Flour 104
Garlic 25, 30, 36,
45, 46, 49,
56, 63, 91,
99, 100,
107, 108,
111, 119,
120, 123,
127, 128,
132, 135,
136, 141,
146, 149,
153, 154,
161, 165,
166
Ginger......................29, 67, 83
- Root 29, 95
Gnocchi 111
Grapefruit 29, 116
Hazelnut 25, 68,
193
- Milk 35
- Oil 56
Heavy Cream................50, 100,
145
Hemp Oil 35, 36,
56, 84
Honey 50, 60, 68,
115, 127,
131, 173,
174, 182,
185, 189
Italian Bread Crumbs....119
Jicama 59
Juniper Berries............115
Kalamata Olives 60, 111,
150
Kale Leaf...................115
Leek Stalk..................145
Lemon 25, 36, 45,
84, 123,
145, 174
- Juice 35, 45, 46,
50, 55, 56,
59, 60, 63,
64, 67, 68,
99, 104,
115, 120,
131, 145,
149, 150,
154, 161,
162, 165,
173, 177,
181, 182,
185, 186

- Sorbet 181
Lettuce.....................56, 79
Mango 39, 17
- Juice 178, 1
Maple Syrup.................182, 1
Marjoram....................84, 11
169
Mayonnaise.................63, 64,
79, 92,
Nutmeg......................40, 17
Olives 60, 71,
150, 1
Olive Oil 25
- Extra Virgin.............55, 56,
60, 63,
67, 68,
75, 79,
83, 87
91, 95,
103, 10
108, 12
123, 12
128, 13
132, 14
142, 14
150, 15
154, 15
161, 16
165, 16
Onion.......................25, 30,
88, 91,
- Spanish..................45, 84,
100, 10
108, 11
119, 12
136, 14
146, 14
154, 16
- Vidalia Onions..........128, 12
162, 16
Orange......................68
- Peel.....................29, 36
- Juice 50, 17
181, 18
189, 19
- Zest 29, 17
181, 18
189, 19
193
Oregano.....................150
Papaya......................189
- Papya Juice 29
Parsnips 135
Passion Fruit 39
Pasta
- Gluten-free..............49, 60
- Linguine.................161
- Penne....................161
- Semolina.................149
- Tortellini...............49
- Ziti.....................49
Peanut Butter..............26
Peanut Oil.................75, 15
Peas........................46, 104
111

Snow.....................59
ppers.....................154
Green.....................132
Red.....................166
Yellow.....................132, 166
ppermint.....................177
sto.....................80, 88, 92, 104
ckle.....................76, 79
ne Nuts.....................104, 107, 119, 127, 154, 185
heapple.....................131, 181, 182, 190
stachios.....................56
megranate
Juice.....................40, 127
Seeds.....................68, 71
rt Wine.....................158
rtobello Mushroom..91
tato.....................111
osciutto.....................79, 150
dicchio.....................120
isins.....................173
padura.....................29, 190
d Beet.....................60, 146
d Cabbage.....................63
d Peppercorns.....................104, 135
ce Cake.....................26
ce Milk.....................35, 36
padura.....................29, 190
spberries.....................173, 193
e Pear.....................29
semary.....................103
ge Leaves.....................100
lsa.....................88
rdines.....................95
usage
Beef.....................99
Chicken.....................132, 166
Pork.....................99
Turkey.....................99, 108, 136
allops.....................116
same Seeds.....................84
allot.....................91, 103, 111, 127, 131, 132, 145, 166
iitake Mushrooms.....91, 162
hoked Salmon.....................83, 95, 165
le.....................119, 169
ur Cream.....................55, 103
y Milk.....................35, 36
earmint.....................177
inach.....................49, 55, 63, 71, 76, 84, 87, 95, 99, 108, 116, 123, 131, 132, 135, 145, 166
lk Burdock Root.....100
awberries.....................36, 40, 50, 178
uash.....................56, 84, 99, 100, 103, 107

Sunflower Oil.....................25, 30, 45, 46, 49, 75, 79, 88, 91, 92, 99, 100, 103, 107, 108, 111, 115, 119, 120, 123, 127, 128, 131, 132, 135, 136, 141, 142, 145, 146, 149, 150, 161, 166, 169
Swiss Chard Leaf.....................83, 115
Tarragon.....................119, 123
Thyme.....................115, 150, 165
Tomato.....................45, 46, 75, 79, 111, 153
 - Cherry.....................56, 83, 103, 136, 165
 - Plum.....................49, 67, 104
 - Strawberry Candy.....141
 - Sun-dried.....................100, 154
 - Yellow.....................119
Tofu.....................30, 76, 83
Tofurky.....................128,
Tuna Steak.....................120, 123
Turkey.....................76, 83, 87, 88, 127, 128, 132
Turmeric.....................83
Vanilla
 - Bean.....................50, 182, 193
 - Powder.....................186, 193
 - Yogurt.....................50
Vegetable Broth.....................46, 49, 99, 103, 107, 108, 115, 119, 123, 132, 135, 136, 149, 161
Vegetable Ravioli.....................108
Walnut.....................25, 123, 154
Watermelon.....................177
White Truffle Oil.....................64
Yogurt.....................50
Zucchini.....................80, 159

Author's Notes

In closing, I think anyone can learn to cook. You don't need to become a chef, have expensive tools or a large kitchen. You need to be open to experimenting with food.

If this book has changed the way you eat, the way you cook, or even the way you think about food, then I accomplished what I set out to do! Thank you for purchasing my book.